REBEL
FOR THE
HELL OF IT

REBEL
FOR THE
HELL OF IT

the life of tupac shakur

armond white

THUNDER'S MOUTH PRESS
NEW YORK

Published by
Thunder's Mouth Press
632 Broadway, Seventh floor
New York NY 10012

Interior Design by Pauline Neuwirth, Neuwirth & Associates, Inc.

Library of Congress Cataloging in Publication Data
White, Armond
    Rebel for the hell of it : the life of Tupac Shakur / by Armond White. — 1st ed.
      p. cm.
    Discography: p.
    Includes index.
    ISBN 1-56025-122-0
    1. Shakur, Tupac. 1971-   . 2. Rap musicians—United States—Biography. I. Title.
ML420.s529W55 1997
782.421649'092—dc21
    [B]   96-53671
                                                                  CIP
                                                                  MN

Manufactured in the United States of America.
First Edition

The Publisher wishes to acknowledge Matthew Trokenheim for his
dedication, diplomacy, and finely-tuned editorial skills;
Marilyn Wright for her editorial vision; and
Barbara J. Zitwer, a consummate agent
without whom this book would not have happened.

CONTENTS

EDITOR'S NOTE

MARILYN WRIGHT

think big. big lights! Big names! Big cars!
Big jewelry! Big events!

That's the way it was on the night of September 7, 1996. The fabled lights of Las Vegas were ablaze in the desert. The much touted Tyson\Sedon Heavyweight Championship fight at the MGM Grand Hotel had lasted all of two minutes in which a multimillion dollar purse was lost and won. A rising star, Tupac was riding high on the 3 million copy sales of *All Eyez on Me,* his latest double album. He had two new films showcasing his growing skill as an actor in the can, awaiting release. The power and clout of Death Row Records had seemingly ensured his future and he was headed—with Death Row CEO "Suge" Knight— to stage a highly publicized anti-gang youth event at Knight's Club 662. Riding in the passenger seat of a BMW 750 black sedan with an entourage of ten cars behind him, Tupac might have felt like he owned the night until the white Cadillac pulled up beside them at a stoplight and fired a volley of shots, four of which found their mark in Tupac—two of them fatally.

What happened? If anyone knows, they're not telling. No license plate number. No faces. There were ten cars right behind the BMW. According to Kevin Powell's account in *Rolling Stone,* within the next ten minutes, twenty police officers were on the scene, yet no one had a single clue that would point to a shooter. According to yet another account, there was one witness who claimed to have seen something, but by the time the police seriously considered questioning him, some many months later, he was hiphop history—gunned down in a Newark housing project. A trail gone dead cold and silent as the grave.

In the aftermath, a great deal of speculation focused on the East Coast/West Coast "rap war" born of legendary bad blood between Tupac and Biggie Smalls. For a time this "war" had seemed good publicity for both sides, whatever the truth of it. Tupac had publicly denied it was anything more than business rivalry. But had the sweet taste of real success turned it truly deadly serious?

While the notion of strike-back revenge hovered in the air, the answer seemed to come up a likely *No* on the night that New York's star rapper Biggie Smalls— born Christopher Wallace and alternatively known as The Notorious B.I.G.—left a celebrity bash in L.A. shortly after midnight.

With a front guard of friends and a rear guard of security personnel, Biggie got as far as Fairfax and Wilshire before a dark sedan pulled alongside and someone began firing a 9mm weapon. Biggie was declared dead on arrival at Cedars-Sinai Hospital less than an hour later. According to Cheo Hodari Coker's account in *Vibe,* LAPD officers gave chase but came back without so much as a license plate number. It was almost six months to the day Tupac Shakur had died, gunned down in Vegas.

Such flamboyant lives. Such flamboyant waste. Tupac was twenty-five;

Biggie was twenty-four. In another world—a mainstream, middle-class world—they could be seen as little more than brash boys, gifted young men with fabulous showbiz careers ahead of them. In their own world, twenty-five was seen by many as the outer limits of longevity. And it was *that* world their music came from—a world of raw experience, of street life, of sex and drugs, of down-and-dirty despair igniting into incendiary defiance that all too often found it's expression in deadly violence. Once it's meistersingers had hit the charts and put big money in their pockets, they had no choice but to leave those wild streets behind them. But in that their art was fashioned from those streets, and rebelliously denied any need or wish to melt into the monied American mainstream, just where were they to go? With all that high-flying cash and celebrity jazz, the very streets they rapped about were no longer safe for them to walk..or even drive. A painful paradox. An enigma. And a mystery.

Why did they die? Was it the violence of the music, the glorification of the gun leading to death by the gun—the gangster in *gangsta rap* coming home to roost? Certainly their angry message found an eager audience, tapped into heated energies that it did not invent and gave voice to rage that might never have escaped the inner cities whose life inspired it. Was the music itself a vent for explosive emotions that might have found a more political outlet in simpler times or did it merely draw violent energy to those who sang its tune, escalating that violence until it imploded...a cautionary tale for our troubled time?

Suge Knight—the dark knight who had sprung Tupac from the slammer on over $1 million dollar bail and brought him into the creative, protective fold of Death Row Records— is now in jail himself, serving a nine-year sentence for assorted weapons and assault charges. Even in jail, he has been in protective custody, guarded from Los Angeles gang members, Cripps and Bloods who some think may have had a hand in the drive-by shootings. Although Knight has tried to keep things going, California law prohibits prisoners from running businesses from the jailhouse. So Norris Anderson, Suge's general manager and brother-in-law, holds the fort, along with David Kenner, Suge's lawyer, who has, according to *Vibe*'s Rob Marriott, built a lucrative and powerful practice defending some of the country's most infamous drug lords. Then, there are law suits over broken contracts, unpaid rent, and Knight and Kenner's now infamous $1.5 million dollar American Express bill, all of which apparently forced Suge to mortgage millions of dollars in assets—including mastertapes and artists' contracts—to Interscope, to keep Death Row Records afloat. There are claims that notorious drug kingpin Michael Harris a.k.a. Harry-O had a founding interest in Death Row, and rumors of other, more far-reaching underworld connections. There are memories of powerful politicos—beginning with Dan Quayle—who came out openly against rap's message and exerted considerable pressure to end mainstream sponsorship of rap labels—despite their spectacular profitability.

And beyond all of this, there is Afeni Shakur, Tupac's mother, activist and spokesperson of 60s Panther fame, struggling with the legalities which might explain why Tupac died owing Death Row $4.9 million, despite having sold $60 million worth of records in the year before his death alone. As her brother-in-law, stepfather to her children, and fellow Panther Mutulu Shakur, after twenty-five years in prison, faces the possibility of release on the basis of "new evidence" which points to his innocence, Afeni is trying to understand why—despite Tupac's fabulous success—her son died apparently owning nothing. . .not the Rolls Royce he drove—not even their home.

The mystery behind Tupac's death—and Biggie Small's—reeks of dangerous secrets, the kind of secrets that would prompt one to say—if one knew, "We could tell you—but then we'd have to kill you." (A joke, but one that's made more and more often these days.) Two more murders of public figures, committed in full public view, in which no one, apparently, knew, saw, or heard anything that could point to a killer. An All-American tradition. The All-American way.

But that is not what this book is about. That is where it appears to end but not where it begins. This book is about where it all began.

This book is about the forces—intimately personal, political, sociological, and musical—that brought Tupac Shakur, child of intellectually astute, revolutionary Black Panther parents, to that fatal stoplight in the city of money and lights where his own star, encrusted with diamonds, glittering with heavy gold, was—for a brief moment—ablaze in the night. It is an exploration of the factors that led him away from the bold and direct political activism his parents embraced into the glare of another spotlight that focused, in part, on communal problems, but more particularly on the narcissistically personal—and even grandiose—life of the star performer.

It is an exploration of pop music that begins with the revolutionary changes in the 60s, leaps into rock and Motown, and leads to the curious mutation that gave birth to rap in the 80s and 90s. From the Temptations to Snoop Doggy Dog, Dr. Dre, The Notorious B.I.G., and Tupac himself, it seeks to put rap in its larger musical context as an expression of a people, a culture, and a time.

It is an exploration of pop culture—of kids growing up bombarded by media which shape their dreams and ambitions for better or for worse. . .of defiant poorboy ghetto culture seeking to be heard, to make its mark in an exploitative culture where big money has the last word.

It is a rags to riches story with a tragic ending that casts an oblique and deeply disturbing light on the complex values of the 90s. A rags to riches story that illuminates the life of Tupac Shakur, with all its high-flying triumphs as well as its considerable flaws and failings. . .the story of a complex young man of many talents who lived with an almost mythical drive and energy. . . who sought but never found the elusive balance between the material success he craved and the wrenching racial/cultural issues he was born to who seized a voice for himself and dreamed of speaking for his people. . .who found—by sheer talent and daring—an enduring place in the the hearts of millions.

parental advisory

REBEL FOR THE HELL OF IT *was written before the March 19, 1997 killing of The Notorious B.I.G. I let all comment on that artist stand as proof of the significance he shared with Tupac in representing the picture of hiphop. I also want to remind all those hiphop exploiters who claimed the rationale behind the 1992 Los Angeles uprising as already in the music, to keep rap in the perspective it deserves. Pious moralizing about the violent deaths of Tupac and Biggie Smalls suggests that many people still don't take the music seriously. Had they really comprehended hiphop, they would have expected these rappers to die horribly, suddenly, predictably. Tupac and Biggie weren't clairvoyant but they were part of a cultural system that dangerously capitalizes on Black talent while undervaluing Black life.*

INTRODUCTION

tears twinkled like stars in Afeni

Shakur's eyes as she told a TV interviewer of her son's death struggle:

The doctor came out and said that Tupac had stopped breathing. Three times. And they had revived him three times. And that every time they revived him, he just went back. And I asked them to leave him alone and to let him go. I really felt it was important for Tupac, who fought so hard to have a free spirit. I thought it was important for his spirit to be allowed to be free. And so I rejoiced with him and the release of his spirit. I rejoiced then, and I rejoice now when I'm not crying...

Afeni did not cry alone. Hiphop followers around the world mourned the death of one of pop music's most charismatic stars. Tupac's first two albums *2pacalypse Now* and *Strictly for My N.I.G.G.A.Z.* each sold enough copies to qualify for Gold Record status; his third, *Me Against the World*, reached that level within its first year of release; and each of his subsequent albums debuted in the Number One chart position with the posthumous Makaveli album, *The Don Killuminati The Seven-Day Theory*, selling over 600,000 copies within its first week of release. Soaring record sales signify an eager, committed audience—a level of fan devotion that, in itself, affirms Tupac's importance in pop music and in the hearts of those who responded to his art.

Those hearts were broken by two events in the fall of 1996.

First, on September 7th, when Tupac was shot in Las Vegas. He had just seen Mike Tyson's Heavyweight Championship fight. Tyson and Tupac—both recently jailed pop icons—had shared ideas on improving their social status. After the fight, Tupac rode in a white limousine with Marion "Suge" Knight, his new mentor and owner of Death Row records, heading for Knight's Club 662 to celebrate Tyson's victory as their own. Earlier that evening, leaving the fight, Tupac and Knight had been involved in a brief scuffle. Now, on Flamingo Road, their caravan of six cars stopped at a red light. A white Cadillac pulled up alongside, a man got out , walked over to Tupac's window and shot. Tupac took four bullets—he wasn't wearing his usual protective bulletproof vest—and Knight was grazed. Ambulances rushed Tupac to University Medical Center.

Second heartbreak: On September 13th, Tupac died. Cause of death: respiratory failure. Doctors had removed one lung to assist his breathing; but the internal bleeding continued. After a week of intensive, critical care, including a medically-induced coma, the rapper's fight ended.

But Tupac's memory plays on for audiences in search of a voice and as a figure expressing their impatience and anger: the son of Black activists and a potent force in one of the most exciting cultural movements of the last two decades. With the devolution of social ideals in an era of naked, shameless, brutal exploitation, Tupac created a body of work that spoke from all sides of the times' confusion. When Tupac's passion left the earth, loving listeners could, like Afeni, rejoice that he no longer suffered the indignity of laboring under hiphop's shrill corporate take-over—a development that denied his ideals of individual revolution and demanded that listeners and artists alike exchange their deepest feelings for marketplace value.

Tupac's achievement as a pop artist was based on notions of unruly behavior that had once seemed revolutionary but in an era of compromise, became as common as everyday frustration and the endless search for pleasure and joy. The logical outcome of those notions was largely embodied by Tupac's own fate, and tragically acted out by his assassination, his disparagement, his death, his suppression—the four bullets fired, as so often in today's tragic tales, by a "brother."

We lost Tupac before he died. His embodiment of reckless Black defiance delighted hiphop heads while they thrilled to such popular tunes as "California Love," "Keep Your Head Up," and "Dear Mama," the imperishable story of a son's love for his mother's strength, but mostly for her ideas (it's in the groove). Not much pride in his achievement or family concern over his self-destructive acts was voiced while Tupac lived—only a few cautionary observations from the sidelines and an occasional pat on the head, such as distracted parents, totally taken up by their own woes, are wont to give. And so Tupac bequeathed to the hiphop nation the same contradictory bluster that he could depend on to get attention and win recognition. Like the late rap impresario Eazy E (Eric Wright), Tupac has left behind complicated legacies of thuggishness/caring, seriousness/silliness, affection/crime, sex/violence and through it all, pride. Tupac's paradoxes stand right next to the defilement that mainstream media sponsor for Black people and the celebration of success that many Black folks, following the dictates of the Reagan era, respect as much as personal integrity.

Sentiment swelled for Tupac's death-defying conduct and this well-meant indulgence, in part, prevented him from receiving the good counsel and safe company that might have kept him alive. Thus his reputation and, most importantly, his *effect*, grows. This is the crossroads—not the same as Robert Johnson's legendary place of decision, but the everyday, common choice Black folks have to determine their lives rigorously or carelessly.

Tupac's death raises questions about the future of Black popular music and the roles that musicians and the music industry play in sustaining a discussion of contemporary social problems and human potential. Not only are these the basic themes in rap music—behind the scenes dramas of gang wars, drug-selling, sexual competition—but they are the very issues at the heart of Shakur's life and art.

Tupac's embrace of the hard stance, the wild movement, the behavioral extreme—explained by his various hot justifications—were part of a disintegrating moral center. Young folks, already disillusioned, had begun to slip through the cracks. As old-fashioned social remedies lost their possibilities and appeal, the young also lost their elders' sympathy. A moral impasse resulted.

If such a thing as middle-aged rap artists existed, there might be records dealing with this new, lost-generation phenomenon. The closest I can come is British singer Morrissey's 1992 "The National Front Disco," with its canny lamentation: *"Where is our boy?/ Oh, we've lost our boy!/ But I should know/ Where you've gone/ Because again and again you've explained."* Tupac's anger fits those lines; and the next account for his reasons: *"There's a country/ You don't live there/ But one day you would like to/ And then you'll show them what you're made of/ Oh, then you might do."*

Morrissey's controversial song has gotten as little sympathetic scrutiny as Tupac—even in England—because it requires a bold confrontation with the fact of social unrest and the desperate quest for a sense of purpose. Black American pop fans hardly crossed over to Morrissey's playlist, but ironically they might have been his most perceptive audience.

Tupac represents the most alarming characteristics of that song—the dislocation felt by people estranged from the circumstances they were born into. As a result, unwise, faulty, dangerous choices are made by young people desperate for answers. Earlier generations might have known how to react, following traditional routes of revolt and protest, but in the past twenty years protest has lost its luster and aspiration has become embarrassing—except when the goal is money. "Cash rules everything around me," as Wu-Tang Clan say in "C.R.E.A.M."

Black American youth, probably more so than the British disenfranchised, felt additional weight from the race-based system of oppression and discouragement. By the early nineties, the harm of that system was extensive though increasingly disavowed by the mainstream. Meanwhile, social options for Black youth decreased, even the possibility for effective rebellion. Thus, in both American and British youth culture, two types of youth emerged: the capitalist and the social renegade (which would include a lower order apostate, the slacker). Neither group was mutually exclusive—they'd all been raised believing in the power of the capitalist state—and the music industry made profitable fodder of them all. Our loss of Tupac has much to do with the way an industry could deceive him and his peers by manipulating them in such a way as to simultaneously appease their political desperation and their material yearning?

Miscomprehension, another modern epidemic, explains how both Tupac could appall and distance people. Jailed activist Sanyika Shakur, writing about Tupac's death, used a superb word—"overstand"—that gets us close to penetrating such pop culture alarm. "Overstand" challenges the ideology we take for granted in the word "understand" by asserting the command of ideas over established rules and law. While Tupac and Morrissey represent contrasting responses to social ills, the questions they raise require pop audiences to think for themselves about the personal pain of social distress. Tupac put it succinctly when he worried, "Will I die if I don't go pop?" on the album *All Eyez on Me*.

To *overstand* Tupac's life and career means seeing through the strategems of corporate exploitation as well as the myths of Black consciousness that the rapper himself could never reconcile, perhaps, because he thought he *under-stood* them so well.

As Russell Simmons eulogized in *The Source*, "Tupac wasn't headed for this anymore than, say, Sean Penn or Kurt Cobain. It was just that rebellious-ness for the sake of it, that wild Rock-n-Roll side of him, that did this. The atti-tude in our world, especially in youth culture, promotes all of this."

This book is an attempt to make sense of "all of this"—Tupac and the con-text in which he lived. Unsettled by the mass atonement occasioned by that par-ticular driveby shooting, I mourn for the meanings lost to those people who either follow or distrust Black culture. To overstand ignorance, I have attempt-ed a study of Tupac's art/life (not mutually exclusive). He belonged to a great period in American cultural history and his art/life makes the most sense when viewed through the auspicious moment that is hiphop.

It's easy to say "Fuck you!" There's no swifter mechanism for social defense; every person who lives Black in America needs to keep a "fuck you" in his back pocket. But when that handy phrase doesn't get you what you need, it's time for strategy, which means contemplation. And that's what distinguishes the richest rap songs from the simplest ones. Rebelling for the hell of it means say-ing "Fuck you," but in taking the leap from revolutionary ambition to thug life, Tupac proved it was never enough. In 1995 he said, "I'm going to save these young niggas because nobody else wants to save them. Nobody ever came to save me. They just watch what happen to you. That's why Thug Life to me is dead. If it's real, then let somebody else represent it, because I'm tired of it." And yet, when posing for the cover of *All Eyez on Me*, he threw up a 'W' hand sign to taunt East Coast-West Coast rivalry, then claimed, "It's a W for war!"

If it helps to mend that terrible, unnecessary rift, I have taken *Ready to Die*, the debut album by The Notorious B.I.G., as a model. Deep down, despite his differences with Biggie Smalls, Tupac loved that album which sums up the hiphop aesthetic. It's insight and wit caught Tupac's attention. And that fasci-nation is correct, a reason to come together if only upon reflection. *Ready to*

Die's vision of life is movie-style vivid. The opening cut sets up a hiphop biography. A child—Biggie's—birth surprises its young parents whose joy doesn't last long. The sound of labor pains recalls the birth description in Ice Cube's "The Product"- " *And it was hell tryin' to bail to the ovary/ With nothin' but the Lord lookin' over me/ I was white with a tail/ But when I reached the finish line/ YOUNG BLACK MALE!*"

But Biggie doesn't start off so cynically; there's comforting, resonant Black pop in the background at different stages of the youngster's life:

BIRTH: Curtis Mayfield's "Superfly"
SCHOOL MISCHIEF/PARENTAL FIGHT: "Rapper's Delight"
SUBWAY MUGGING: Audio Two's "Top Billin'"
JAIL RELEASE: Snoop's "Gin and Juice"

Tupac admired the way Biggie kept pace with the historical development of Black pop, showing rappers' engagement with the form and the music's connection to real life. The seventies' notion of using music as a soundtrack to life is trashed here by a deeper, more interesting analogy that takes the message, the tone, the feel of pop—not as background or foreground but as *expression*. This may be a particular feeling of the hiphop generation, whose modern experience is both defined and substantiated by pop music and the culture surrounding it.

Subsequently, the updating track, "Things Done Changed," beautifully shades nostalgia with a palpable series of harp arpeggios conveying how pop permeates emotion. Each track on *Ready to Die* can be taken as a piece of the world—a piece of hiphop itself. Turned on to his culture, Biggie becomes a part of it. And that's what this book is intended to do: it's implicit narrative confirms that the topics of hiphop records—crime, anger, sex, dope (what, no politics?)—are also the real stuff of rappers' lives (thus politics). Proof comes through the imaginative production, vibrant lyrics, and the profane but fully engaged voices of both Tupac and Biggie.

Similarly, Tupac needs to be situated among the records, movies, plays, and other cultural events that taught him how to think about the world and how to talk about his place in it. Chapter by chapter, *Rebel For the Hell of It* moves through the events in Tupac's art and life, shifting like a CD changer, from the ambitions of his adolescence as a drama student in Baltimore, to the more important story of his parents' political legacy and the music culture that expressed it. Tupac's migration to Northern California is followed by an explanation of his ideological upbringing in Chapter Four. Tupac's first album and his first film are detailed; then the self-assessment in relation to his hiphop peers that began with his second album. Chapter Eight examines Tupac's experience as a cultural icon, followed by the souring events in Hollywood during the filming of *Poetic Justice*. Chapter Ten focuses on Tupac's mounting legal hassles that are next amplified by the retorts he recorded in *Me Against the World*. Chapter Eleven examines the history behind his most beloved song, "Dear Mama," his growing reputation in the world of hiphop, the moral temptation and infatuation with criminal insolence that brought him to Death Row's door. Chapter Fifteen, beginning with discussion of his two-disc epic *All Eyez On Me*, covers the final year of Tupac's life. Next, the double consciousness of Tupac's Makaveli alter-ego is examined, followed by his posthumous image in mainstream media. We conclude with Tupac's efforts to create a permanent hiphop asthetic on screen and give final consideration to the moral and political stakes he raised.

In constructing this critical biography, I want to acknowledge the chronicling by *Right On!, Word Up!, The Agenda,* and other publications that have covered hiphop with the faith that the music told a larger story. I hope my regard does justice to the art and to the people who love it. These would include the lifesavers behind this book, Eric Lawrence and Dennis Myers. Extra encouragement came from Richard Hecht, who showed patience, Gregory Solman, Benj DeMott and Jerry Green. And thanks to Keith Gardner and Robert Lazzaro. I gratefully dedicate this book to young people, Tupac fans or not, who keep widening their perspectives: Teofilo Colon and my other nieces and nephews.

ARMOND WHITE

CHAPTER 1

memories of overdevelopment

"i want to be a revolutionary!" ten-year-old Tupac told Reverend Herbert Daughtry. Not too many years later, Tupac's yearning would take him to acting school where his radical zeal would be encouraged. But as a respectful youngster, mindful of his elders, Tupac answered Daughtry's inquiry about his ambitions boldly, with all the self-assurance of a prodigy. Revolutionary status was his goal. It was the early eighties and attending Daughtry's The House of the Lord Church in Brooklyn, New York, with his mother Afeni and his sister Asantewaa, gave Tupac a traditional African American grounding, part of the upbringing that many Black families felt necessary to establish moral boundaries and encourage stable goals for their children.

The gospel quote, "Teach a child the way that he should go; and when he is old he shall not depart from it," is a familiar axiom of Black American family life. Anyone who has listened to the records Tupac made as a rap artist can hear "the way that he should go" echoing gospel oral tradition. Rap's exceptional verbal command also indicates familiarity with—and indoctrination in—methods of articulation and, especially, the command of emotional sincerity. Tupac learned in church how to mean what you say. In answering Reverend Daughtry's inquiry about his future by aspiring to be "a revolutionary," he knew his reply would provoke a surprised but approving response. A boy courts the favor of an adult by exemplifying and repeating their own pet notions. Daughtry's pastoral had long advocated community action and boldness. Seeing his own enthusiasms reflected back to him in a shining, earnest young face, placed Daughtry among Tupac's very first audiences.

At the September 20, 1996 memorial service held for Tupac at The House of the Lord Church, Reverend Daughtry recounted that moment mournfully:

"Afeni brought him, along with his sister Asantewaa to this holy place. The three of them stood right there at the altar and united with this congregation. He was a lad of about 10 years. When I asked him what he wanted to be he replied, 'a revolutionary.' Needless to say, I was surprised. I ought not to have been. There is a saying concerning 'a chip off the old block,' and 'the twig doesn't fall far from the tree.' His mother, Afeni, who was pregnant with him while incarcerated for allegedly plotting to bomb something—later found not guilty—was a revolutionary. She was a member of the Black Panther Party, a group of young Black men and women who, some years ago, created enormous fear among some whites and a certain kind of Black.

"Afeni was committed to making things better for the masses. She was a revolutionary. If revolution means complete change, she wanted that. Afeni wanted a complete change for the better and she thought that could happen with the Black Panthers. Later she was to fall on hard times, but we are not here to tell her story. We're here to remember Tupac. Tupac, the revolutionary. He said 'I want to be a revolutionary.' Maybe that explains his life."

ARMOND WHITE

Daughtry's eulogy gave religious and political parallels that may be as important to consider in searching for an understanding of Tupac's young life as any of its more mundane incidents. The boy absorbed the idea of revolution as a goal much the way Sunday School students absorb the Ten Commandments; but Tupac kept his eyes on a worldly prize with almost equal religious zeal.

"After he joined the church, " Daughtry continued. "He played as any normal child. He laughed. He cried. He played with other children." But it was a childhood resonant with the contradictions—the joys and woes—of a changing America. A revolution was taking place quietly in Tupac's head and the world around him, a revolution unlike any Afeni would have sanctioned.

In 1981, as the Reagan Era's mean-spirited policies began polarizing the nation between power and poverty, Afeni sought the ministry of an activist preacher like Daughtry. She knew her young warrior would need a double-tiered spiritual education. Daughtry knew his way around the community structures of Black Brooklyn: how to use the media to expose his congregation's problems and provoke a response to their needs. He would be pleased to find a young parishioner who also seemed to have his mind on change.

Although the seventies had been relatively complacent, Black America found itself confronting new social challenges that threatened to reignite the activism and rage that had exploded in the sixties. Young Tupac's dream of revolution stood out—a rare raised fist amongst the millions of kiddie hands clutching Pac-Man joysticks. His answer to Rev. Daughtry reflects Afeni's experience and her soberly-adjusted attitude toward social change—his mother's son's loyalty mixed with an early sense of inherited mission. A child of the revolution that never got televised, Tupac Amaru—which translates as "shining serpent," a reference to an insurrectionist Incan warrior (the Arabic name "Shakur" means "Thankful to God.")—was part of the new generation who were given Afrocentric names but would have to search long and hard for their emotional identities in an era of unprecedented turmoil and temptation. The claim Tupac made to Daughtry was a testament to his role-models; the revolutionary idea had gotten through to him despite the eighties' general emphasis on accommodation and reward.

Tupac listened, observed and absorbed. His bright eyes reflected a generation alert to the culture and the times. What he sensed was the skid that was taking place on the road to social equity. When Ronald Reagan smashed the air traffickers strike, his unprecedented action sent a shudder through a people brought up to believe in ideas of fair wages, worker's integrity, and the hope that the unions had represented for more than five decades. A new desperation was creeping in. Something cold was undercutting the hot passions of righteous activism that had inflamed the previous generation of Black youth, tempering the lessons Afeni exemplified and that Daughtry endowed with higher moral purpose. Afeni's dreams—like the beliefs of so many parents teaching their children through the mythology of ideas to help them make sense of everyday endeavors and set-backs—were being undermined by a coarsening social temper.

One of the delusions of the Dr. Spock generation is that children can be sheltered from the world's harsh and bewildering realities. But the surprising candor and realism heard in many rap records prove otherwise—a child's sensitive awareness is part of growing up. Information about the world is pointlessly hidden because children will seek it out and the world imposes its hard truths anyway. Through shared language and daily media bombardment, American childhood is imprinted with the spirit of the times. To an individual for whom all things are new, an amoral education takes place, jumbling sentimental notions with brutal logic to create an image of the way the world works.

Childhood pleasure dukes it out with practicality. It can be unnerving or fulfilling to imagine how a child will acquire the necessary balance. During daily subway rides and walks through New York, the sight of homelessness, deprivation, and violence prompted Tupac to ask his mother "Why?" Afeni's replies must have been tempered to instill hope as well as resolve; she needed to give her child a sense of worth, balancing the joy they found among family and friends with the encroaching poverty and problems of post-Panther life.

Probably the only child who understands the relation between pleasure and struggle is an artistic child. Observing the aggression and rage, the high-voltage tension that makes all frenzy seem natural or, at the very least, inescapable—Tupac may have been affected by New York City but it was theater school that shaped his intensity. Exposure to expressive arts gave reign to Tupac's imagination and to the dramatization of whatever impulses, convictions or confusions he felt.

Afeni enrolled Tupac in a Harlem theater group, The 127th Street Ensemble. At age 12, his first performance took place at the Apollo Theater in a production of Lorraine Hansberry's play about a Black Chicago family planning to escape urban poverty by moving to an all-white suburb, *A Raisin in the Sun*. Tupac had the kid's role: Travis, the son of Walter Lee Younger, who witnesses the microcosm of Black American social striving. Travis' most important moment paralleled Tupac's own life. When Walter Lee loses the family nest egg and is offered a payoff to stay out of the all-white upscale community, Travis is brought to the center of the family turmoil and silently put in place by his strong-willed grandmother. She demands that the father set an example his son can follow:

"I've come from five generations of people who was slaves and sharecroppers, but ain't nobody in my family never let nobody pay them no money that was a way of telling us he wasn't fit to walk the earth. We ain't never been that poor, We ain't never been that dead inside. No Travis, you stay right here. And you make him understand what you're doing, Walter Lee. You teach him good like Willie Harris taught you. You show where our five generations done come to. Go ahead son.

Such a play—such a moment—forces knowledge on the actor as it does on the audience. Playing Travis added to Tupac's sense of alienation. It gave a deeper purpose to the extracurricular activity of acting, making use of his dawning sense of injustice, leading him to a more serious appreciation of childhood than his street-running peers, who often taunted him for his difference. "This is something that none of them kids can do,'" Tupac proclaimed, proud of his sophisticated skill yet revealing his adolescent pain and uncertainty. "I didn't like my life, but through acting, I could become somebody else."

A southern shift would enhance that perception. In 1985, Afeni moved the family from New York to Baltimore. Hardship instigated the change; there was man trouble and—in the city, itself—the atmosphere of atrophy. As an ex-Panther, Afeni watched through the seventies and into the eighties as conditions for Black America worsened, particularly in New York with its ethnic divisions and municipal power splits that repeatedly excluded Black citizens. Starting out in the Bronx, Afeni shuttled her family from borough to borough; an exasperated Mother Courage, she began to understand the allure that the South held for many northern Blacks. Northern life—with its post-World War II promise of jobs and opportunity—began to pall as the nation changed and the economy supported fewer opportunities to make a working-class living.

Urban Baltimore's large Black population with its unique half-Southern small-town scale, its alternately charged yet slower pace helped soothe the family's agitation. Tupac attended Rolling Park Junior High up to eighth grade, improvising, making the kind of adjustments, and facing the kind of disorientation that army brats experience when their parents are constantly forced to relocate. It was only with Tupac's admittance to the Baltimore School of the Arts that the dreaming young revolutionary found a structured outlet for his energy. In teaching styles of expression, BSA encouraged role-playing and play-acted emotional intensity. Among students, conflicts, infatuations, and a kaleidoscope of identities could be playfully explored, as in games of musical chairs. In contrast to the Bronx's school of swift kicks, Tupac found himself enrolled in what modern America—with its downsizing of federal interest, shrinkage of government funds allocated to education, and massive cutting of school appropriations—would come to see as an increasingly rare opportunity to learn and experiment. His imagination sparked, Tupac's creativity bloomed. "That school was saving me, you know what I'm sayin'? I was writing poetry and shit, and I became known as MC New York because I was rapping and then I was doing the acting thing."

Tupac's rap vocation came as a part of the intensified growth spurt that many contemporary teens were experiencing. This was also a period of grassroots renaissance in those northeastern enclaves like The Bronx and New Jersey where rap began. A Baltimore friend was fatally shot while playing with guns— a now frequent gun-culture tragedy but, at the time, the start of a dread new reality spreading through American cities. Part of what gave hiphop its appeal was its recognition of such savage realities. The mainstream rarely recognized or tried to make sense of the drugs and violence sweeping the inner cities. It would take a cultural revolution like hiphop—with Black kids putting their daily lives into their own words and music—to express this disturbing new reality. It was an experience that only Martin Scorsese, in his 1969 film *Who's That Knocking at My Door,* had touched on before when he portrayed a roomful of fitful young (white) men tossing a loaded weapon among themselves in a slow-motion orgy of danger and risk as the camera tracks the abject fear or hilarity of relief on each face. In that movie, Scorsese anticipates the complexities of rap and hiphop—culture spiked with hazardous social rituals—the compulsion to flaunt arms—that accrue to urban male adolescence. Musical Dread.

Gun in my hand
Bullets in motion
Crushin' like crumbs
The maniac psycho
Makes all bloods run. . . .

Gun control became the subject of the first rap Tupac performed in Baltimore; he responded in his generation's natural terms but also, for perhaps the only time, his rap accepted the taboos of the older generation. Achieving continuity with adults not only stroked Tupac's young ego; he also took artistic assurance from it. Of this period, he said "It was a whole other experience for me to be able to express myself—not just around black people but also around white people and other kinds of people. It was the freest I ever felt in my life."

The accent was on youth and young people were eager to educate and exploit themselves with all the triumphs and disasters that implies. Tupac's classmates exhibited a singular pride in their ability to signify and vent—a pride tinged with adolescent arrogance. Attending Baltimore School of the Arts after the 1980 release of the film *Fame*, which romanticized the exploits of high school teens at New York's High School of the Performing Arts, must have felt like a journey towards the mecca of all one's desires and ambitions. Encouraged to see themselves as special, these kids got a compounded sense of self-worth from a school that catered to the belief in unique talent.

This was where Tupac met the aspiring actress Jada Pinkett, and where they both began their kindred, life-long careers. As childhood photos attest, Tupac was a darkly handsome boy and Pinkett was a light-skinned beauty. As teens, both Tupac and Pinkett were physically striking. Both had trim figures; both batted long lashes over large, direct-staring eyes that didn't hesitate to meet anyone's gaze. Tupac and Pinkett must have found each other—and a lasting friendship—in that uneasy and conflicted fellowship of adolescent narcissism and self-regard. In the way Tupac's motor constantly seemed to be running and in the snapping alertness that makes Pinkett a riveting, if not always convincing, actress, they invented their own street stardom. Playing an odd riff on Muhammad Ali's '60s pride, they created a new, hiphop style centered on perpetual preening whether there was a party, a class-exercise, a stage competition or not.

This intensely social exercise in self-testing, self-consciousness, and self-promotion is part of the universal teenage experience—a transition wherein the dull familiarity of family life is traded for the excitement of new friends, world-

ARMOND WHITE

liness, and independence. For Tupac, this meant a respite from his mother's legacy of activism, from the grueling limitations of poverty, and from the shadowy, unreliable male figures darting in and out of his life. Theater—specifically the joy and interplay of performing—offered him a world away from home. Always "on," Tupac could escape the day-to-day trials his mother was facing to support herself and her family. He found independence and flirtation, too.

Tupac and Pinkett paired up remarkably well in this teenage idyll. Both gifted, both extroverted, they could seem to be challenging everyone around them. It's in drama school that one learns to make use of buried insecurities to inspire outsize expression and command attention. Tupac and Pinkett practiced *Fame's* secret motivation: putting impudence on the surface to cover up the fear underneath. Notice—acclaim—is then the reward that bolsters self-confidence. In theater it is not uncommon for such behavior and technique to become the basis for a style. It explains part of what one could call Tupac's and Pinkett's star quality: Out to make something of themselves by any means necessary, their sexuality was joined to will. As sixties student activist Stokely Carmichael defined it: the will not to be deterred.

Some years later, Tupac confided to the European press what those *Fame*-like days were like:

> **I felt like I was out of place. I learned a good admiration for the real world 'cause it was different cultures, different people. I saw females kissing females,**

I felt like I was out of place. I learned a good admiration for the real world 'cause it was different cultures, different people. I saw females kissing females, males kissing males, so it really wasn't a big thing to me later on when everybody was tripping off homosexuality. I already saw that in my school.

males kissing males, so it really wasn't a big thing to me [later on] when everybody was tripping off homosexuality. I already saw that in my school.

Role playing for the young thespian meant learning to trip off certain ideas of Black masculinity, appropriate behavioral tips for the young mover who refuses to be tricked. It's not surprising, then, that Afeni's son should graduate theater school echoing an old defiant spirit that made Carmichael (eventually to take the name Kwame Toure) glad to observe:

> **One of the most promising developments in the nation today is the new mood among Black college students, who have long formed a conservative group with standard Horatio Alger dreams, imitating white America at its worst. Agitation on Black campuses in 1967 was profound and different from that of 1960-61: there is, today, less of a moral and more of a political orientation. Humble appeal is gone; a powerful mood has developed based on a Black consciousness.**

But Tupac's generation—his acting-out class—turned Toure's prophecy upside down. Tupac learned an impatient, multi-source agitation (from both the holy church and the wicked state) that, without a common moral impetus, proved to be political—though, perhaps, not moral: he preferred action; but in action without introspection, agitation turns back on itself. Rebellion for the hell of it. The impulse to speak out and strike out does little to resolve disquiet. It reflects a demand for answers that is inherent in youth's ingenuous bluster and attack, a demand that is all too easily rejected by older listeners who forget their own adolescent anxiety—an adolescence spent in the clearer, more defined, more active, "mo' better" times that rap itself now rhapsodizes on.

Pay attention to what the hiphop generation feels; it's poignantly clear in what they say, even when they say it in ways that confound expectations. Music is the key. Teens' love for rap in the early eighties was indeed special. They had discovered the value of music to express identity and feelings; their own form of theater. But by the mid-nineties hiphop had foundered. The drastic turn towards gangsta had become more of an industry standard than a cultural absolute. Then, a new set of rap songs began to surface, creating a virtual subgenre to the prevailing gangsta fantasy. It clues one in to what may have been going on in Tupac's head during that time between acting school and rap recording.

In the mid-nineties, Tupac, like most of his peer group hiphopheads, grooved to "Reminisce," Ahmad's "Back in the Day," Coolio's "I Remember" and Wu-Tang Clan's "It Was All So Simple," each a nostalgic ode to the rappers' remembered innocence—a not-so-distant anti-youth. These records confessed a heartfelt simplicity at odds with the reckless rage of gangsta rap. Coolio's reference to The Intruders' "Cowboys to Girls" and Wu-Tang Clan's re-working of the Gladys Knight version of "The Way We Were" (released when Tupac and Wu-Tang were pre-schoolers, so it seems like a strain of genetic memory) reveal a sincerity and open-heartedness that is part of these young artists' relationship to the past. Focusing on family cohesion, better days, fun without stress, the songs pose—by sheer contrast—questions about their current lives.

Hiphop nostalgia spins a subtle response to facts of life that may appear harsh and intractable. (Looking back on the North from his new home in Baltimore, Tupac could affirm the sentiment expressed by his buddies in Live Squad's "Heartless" and its memorable line: "See what happens to your life when you're born in New York!") Remembrance of times past and the longing for peace, even if conjured in altered memory—these are feelings Tupac shared. The flavor of '70s Black pop—a generally agreed upon "glory days"—is at the heart of most of these hiphop references. It suggests, "Once there was something better. We *felt* better. Society had not yet abandoned us."

This yearning for what Ahmad calls "the years when I was raised"—what those gruff Wu-Tang adepts recognize as a mere yesterday—differs from the exhaustion of adult nostalgia. It is symptomatic of the unbearable stress young people face today as never before. In appropriately weary realizations, this hiphop idealizes a childhood that never really was, painting the past as positively serene. And because of this, it is possible to understand that hiphop—despite its exaggerated brutishness—contains an effort to retrieve soul. Tupac, the acting student, had to be aware of the motivation to make a value out of what, in modern America, had been deemed inhuman and unsalvageable. As Wu-Tang proves, the hardest kids feel it, even as they recall their strung-out parents' past as the set-up for their own rebellion. Retrieving soul means recollecting something real. The child who attempts to make a new world from his parents' past is a homegrown revolutionary.

CHAPTER 2
rewind to birth

looking back on his early days, Tupac said, "Yeah, we didn't have any lights at home in my house. No lights, no electricity, and 'I'm Bad' by L.L.Cool J. came out and I had batteries in my radio. I heard it for the first time and I was writing rhymes by candlelight and I knew I was gonna be a rapper."

This moment of ironic nostalgia—posing absolute poverty against vaulting ambition—marks a turning point and reveals one crucial source of Tupac's all-or-nothing attitude. California friends have said Tupac loved Ahmad's record "Back in The Day," and cracked a laugh at the lines "I think I was about ten/ One of those happy little niggas singing the blues." It's not just a genre reference or a contradiction; it implies the inheritance not only of a musical style but also an outlook. "Blues" is as much a part of the Black child's experience as playtime possessions concocted from household items.

Ecstasy, security, utopia, revenge—art—is one way to deal with the teenage blues. Tupac had made an unusual trial run towards achieving his high goals at the Baltimore School of the Arts where—as hiphop commanded more of the world's attention, attracting media appreciation and churning up controversy—young folks prepared to shock the world by making art of their lives.

Tupac was seventeen when Public Enemy's *Yo! Bum Rush the Show* and "Bring the Noise," L.L.Cool J.'s *Radio,* and *Bigger and Deffer* made their impact. The advent of rap was an undeniable cultural landmark—a breakthrough. Rap's witty plain-talk on the darkest, deadliest urban woes was what Tupac called "representing the real." To young audiences alienated from mainstream, rap was simply a depiction of the life they knew. A drama student could intuit the relation between this pop revolution and the historical importance of theater. Both arts forms demonstrated ingenuity in addressing listeners, using words and music as their means. Tupac admired hiphop because, like Black theater, it did not seek to please the sophisticated and the snobbish. It was unique in its lack of an authoritarian's voice. It stood for good times, being alive, for doing all the things your parents told you not to. Tupac and his friends thrilled to L.L.Cool J.'s "I'm Bad" for the way it struck a tone that was neither for or against established morality but simply against following anyone else's rules.

Because young Black artists could intuit the potential for a completely new art form in such records as "The Breaks," "The Message," and "Bring the Noise," rap itself would become a theater with enormous appeal, a young person's art form based on young people's relationships and experience. Kids with a sense of the blues were a new audience and gave rap a new social function. Speaking informally, rap commanded language to organize a dramatic form of artist-to-audience communication. Through compelling language and/or the force of the performer's personality, rap shuttled between methods of declaring and confiding its ideas. Rap represented a collective dialogue based on an inner city, insider's understanding—an American kid's inheritance and a soon-to-be accepted theatrical method.

Irresistibly drawn to rap, Tupac was blessed with the ability and energy to imbue his feelings with attractive conviction. His enthusiastic response to the world was forming—adding skillful elocution to impetuous ingenuity. Commanding adolescent lingo and style was just part of it: his energy and personal charm convinced spellbound classmates that a chaotic personality was coherent.

Years later, Tupac used the language of theater to talk about hiphop's uniqueness: "It brought me to myself," he said, as gratefully as an actor describing a Method breakthrough. "Now I have a different philosophy. Hiphop, when it started, it was supposed to be the new thing that had no boundaries and was so different to everyday music. As long as the music has the true to the heart soul, it can be hiphop. As long as it has soul to it, hiphop can live."

There's a blues-like faith in art and principle, a quintessential Black American feeling, but the key to Tupac's appeal is found in his drive and charisma—a personal image that mixes sincerity with truth, cunning with charm, and rebellious anger with acting. Tupac's route from revolutionary to performer is a struggle to summon enough guile, nerve, and enthusiasm to do his Panther legacy—and the secret intelligence of Black show business—proud.

This legacy was passed on by Afeni Shakur, the young woman who joined the Black Panthers in 1968 when she was 22 years old and gave birth to Tupac in a maternity ward of New York University Hospital on June 16, 1971. Only a month before, she had been released from the Women's House of Detention in Greenwich Village after serving time for her suspected part in an alleged Panther plot to bomb banks and department stores. Afeni has spoken passionately about the Tupac pregnancy:

> **I had a million miscarriages, you know. This child stayed in my womb through the worst possible conditions. I had to get a court order to get an egg to eat every day. I had to get a court order to get a glass of milk every day—you**

Panther Minister of Information, Elbert (Big Man) Howard, confers with Panther Afeni Sahkur and Minister of Education, Ray Massi Hewitt.

know what I'm saying? I lost weight, but he gained weight. He was born one month and three days after we were acquitted. I had not been able to carry a child. Then this child comes and hangs on and really fights for his life.

Such intense emotions and motivations are among the revelations of Black American life that the hiphop era has helped make clear. In this case, it reveals Afeni's seemingly paradoxical trust in radical social solutions and divine benevolence.

Tupac's father, Billy Garland, another Panther party member, was not a part of Afeni's life at the time of Tupac's birth (and would not be in Tupac's life for at least 20 years), but both parents knew the tensions of a life that stood in stark contrast to the sanitized image of all-American comfort and contentment. Young Black Americans of that period warmed to political consciousness as an undisputed truth—a cold, clear, *better* way of looking at the world. Their shared optimism and belief that change could be accomplished created a new romanticism. Their vantage point was seventies New York—the Harlem, Brooklyn and New Jersey neighborhoods that made up a New Man's Land of social transition. Decades after the Harlem Renaissance, years after the Black Arts Movement that sparked a sixties upsurge of social beliefs and artistic ambition among New York's intellectuals and urban disenfranchised, that land was succumbing to a wave of desolation that many knew would take desperate measures to stave off. Young people in the early seventies faced truth in the form of a rising national apathy. Making love or having a baby in this climate could seem brave or foolhardy.

Despite their eventual separation, Afeni and Billy Garland were connected by a genuine cultural sensibility. It was the post-riots period when Afeni and Billy met—hearts on fire like Watts, Detroit, and Newark had been—a time when it was possible to fall in love with the buoyancy with which a puffed-out Afro hairstyle was worn or the pride implicit in the way a warrior medallion hung around the neck. Emboldened by the imperatives of the Civil Rights Era that had shown, for almost two decades, how Black Americans deserved equal rights yet had to actively pursue them—perhaps even fight for them, given the stubborn violence of racist tradition—young folks believed they could change things.

This daring move toward change and justice was part of the impulse behind Afeni's interest in the Black Panthers. Started in the late sixties as a grassroots movement in Oakland, California, by two young men—Huey P. Newton and Bobby Seale—the Panthers sought to redress the wrongs suffered from local

Sacramento, CA, May, 2, 1967: Members of the Black Panther Party stand in the corridor of the Capitol in protest of a bill before an Assembly Committee restricting the carrying of arms in public.

police who patrolled their communities like the sentries of an occupying army. The Panthers created a new model of youthful rebellion that spoke to a wearied peoples' frustration and political impatience. Signing on to this resistance movement, Afeni and Billy were drawn toward activist solutions, thus drawn together.

Afeni had already been arrested in 1969 for conspiracy to bomb public places in New York. She began her involvement with Garland while out on bail, also meeting a second man, a local hood known only as "Legs." Whether renegades or criminals, all shared concepts of political truth and social justice. In that churning atmosphere, the pop music boom represented a tidal shift. Every kid whose heart rises to the sound of a particular song on the radio knows the excitement of this kind of culture quake. In the sixties, it happened simultaneously with—and as an expression of—changed social attitudes. From Oakland to Detroit to New York, Huey Newton's arrest could inspire local graffiti artists to spray "FREE HUEY" messages to the world. Likewise, there was a rare enthusiasm in the way a song of this period connected with public feeling, with what young people had in their hearts that the world had previously ignored. The joy of a great song spread across the nation on the heels, toes, snapping fingers and swiveling hips of improvised dance steps.

Along with this musical explosion, new potential shone in the way Berry Gordy, Jr., a young Black entrepreneur, gathered talented young singers and musicians from Detroit's auto factories and public schools and presented them to the public in a corporate parallel to the new Black initiatives of the Civil Rights Movement. When Brenda Evans, Billy Calvin, and Joe Harris—a trio of high school vocalists full of sophomoric effrontery and cleansing, new-broom charm—made it into Motown, they awarded themselves the revolutionary title The Undisputed Truth and launched their debut single, "Smilin' Faces (Sometimes)."

Such an R&B hit contains the substance of a social era as well as a key to understanding the future that derived from it. Hiphop's spiritual and musical origins are as traceable as the romantic and practical origins of Tupac's life. Both can be found in "Smilin' Faces (Sometimes)," a cultural touchstone in 1971. No sensitive, aware young adult could pass through that time and remain unmoved by that song. Number Two on the pop charts, Number One on R&B, it provided a soundtrack—a background for thinking and loving, for being and protesting as idealistic young Afeni and Billy Garland did. Afeni must have been particularly susceptible to musical charm. After all, her parents had christened her Alice Faye Williams, a big-up to the personable, blonde, 1940's band-singer and movie star. (There may be more to be gained from knowing that Afeni came from a background open to the charms of Alice Faye singing "This Year's Kisses" than from a long bland list of parental activities.) Certainly, Afeni was aware of the irony when she changed her name and chose the name of an Incan warrior for her child, choices suggesting matters of cultural affinity and change-able political patterns that go deeper into the essence of Black life than simple bio-graphical detail can impart. American pop history brims with rich paradoxes.

Who could resist The Undisputed Truth? The group's two Black men and one Black woman sang ardor and insight long before The Fugees, a similarly-constituted nineties group, were even gleams in their parents' eyes. Surpassing the simple differences of most coed pop groups, The Undisputed Truth used con-versational interplay both between the sexes and within a community. Singing in whispers, tremors and startled exhortations, they communicated distress, a shared alarm, in which each of the three singers confirms the sadness and the wisdom of the others so that no one of them is ever alone.

A reversal was taking place. Only two years earlier, The Fifth Dimension had retrieved its lost relevance in the ghetto (a word made popular by student activists). They had grabbed it from a distance and with kid gloves, like parv-enues snatching crumbs of soul food from a picnic table as the record compa-ny limousine zoomed them through the inner city en route to the suburbs. There is something genuinely, inherently ethnic in "Stone Soul Picnic"—it evokes family reunion and street corner jive but sung in gospel-like chorale. Part of the wonder of the era was that bourgies could achieve such clout. In the song, those high gloss repetitions of that other newly coined phrase, "soul" (even as Florence La Rue and Marilyn McCoo made each utterance crystalline), sounded authentic. It locked The Fifth Dimension in place as an R&B group. Even radical nationalists got the message of unity in "Stone Soul Picnic's" arch declamations, it being not less authentic of Black experience (precisely, Black career luck) than the way The Undisputed Truth distilled five-part harmonics into three-part sultriness. There's evidence of this style in the way Tupac himself would later trade verses with K-Ci on "I Ain't Mad at Cha," and in the vocals of Bone Thugs-N-Harmony.

Following quickly on Marvin Gaye's landmark 1970 album, *What's Goin' On*, this ethnospecific approach wasn't exactly unheard of, but it had a new feel. Suddenly, The Undisputed Truth was facing up to nihilism, defying it in fascinating, soul-deep ways. By darkening The Fifth Dimension's complacency and glee, their satisfied sense of settling for mainstream America's standards, The Undisputed Truth acknowledged in its stead the acceptance of a bold new standard— a sense of in-your-face reality that opposed middle-class, establishment-pleasing nicety that was the model for The Fifth Dimension's success. The name "Undisputed Truth" presupposes an argument won. It

> . . .the song could be heard as an indicator of underground ruminations and imminent discord.

carries the suggestion of a rebuttal, then dismisses it. Such unfazed debate would have intrinsic appeal to the tense insistence of young activists like Afeni Shakur's Black Panthers, who were used to having their words and deeds disputed by outsiders and, by 1971, from within the ranks. For Afeni, who had distanced herself from Billy Garland when the infatuation faded, turning to other Panther men who came to suit the seriousness of her need, the song could be heard as an indicator of underground ruminations and imminent discord.

Such aggrieved entertainment is one of the defining glories of post-World War II pop culture. "Smilin' Faces (Sometimes)" was co-written by former vocalist Barrett Strong, who sang (and co-penned with Berry Gordy in 1960) Motown's first hit, "Money," the signature ode of urban Black America's strivings. Strong and Gordy were trailblazers at updating blues expressions. One reason there was never a North-South rivalry among sixties Black artists as there was between East-West nineties artists, was the recent memory of what South-to-North migration meant for Black Americans who were simply working at survival wherever they could find a job. A living sense of history bound them. So did respect for the musical interplay heard in superficially diverse "soul" versus "pop" styles. Motown artisans were connoisseurs of blues fundamentals. Knowing that the same American racial experience undergirded both styles, sixties and seventies Black artists left rivalry to journalists and enjoyed the insights pop offered, and the assurance felt from blues resonances. Motown was able to vary Black pop's references by including Northern urbanity in song subjects while keeping Southern vocal depth in the sound of Black pop. By the late sixties, pioneer Strong had begun a songwriting partnership with in-house Motown genius, Norman Whitfield, a collaboration that resulted in at least two masterpieces: The Temptations' "Just My Imagination,"and "Smilin' Faces (Sometimes)."

Whitfield, a producer of exhilarating records, the Hank Shocklee of his day, specialized in rough, atmospheric, almost three-dimensional soundscapes to balance his own melodic romantic tendencies—innate genius checking and balancing the slick technique he developed at Gordy's song factory, dubbed Hitsville, USA. With Strong providing a sturdy yet deluxe shell, Whitfield could experiment with the far side of the Black unconscious—not just proverbial lust and longing, but suppressed rage and despair—and make it go pop. The string glissando on "Just My Imagination" is the sourest irony. It mocks the ecstacy so frequently sung about in Motown hits, especially those nonpareil Smokey Robinson tunes to which The Temptations gave such exquisite voice. By the end of the sixties, Whitfield and Strong had The Temptations earnestly parodying their own winsome selves. "Just My Imagination" remakes Langston Hughes' 1951 "A Dream Deferred" (from the poem "Harlem," which also provided the title for *A Raisin in the Sun)* as if in a Detroit Cadillac plant. Hughes' protest comes off the assembly line sparkling, but revved up with a deeper ache from two more decades of wound, rot, and burden—now ready to explode as his poem predicted. He wasn't just speaking of Black distress but anticipating a culture-wide explosion that Motown ironically named "The Sound of Young America"—the company's brash motto.

"Just My Imagination" turns Black despair into everyone's lament. Disguised as a love song, there is politics in Whitfield-Barrett's deferred dream—the equality struggled for remains just out of reach like an idealized love object. In the early seventies, mention of an unobtainable ideal alluded to so many dissatisfactions and heartaches that each listener could interpret the song in his or her own unique way, while the greater unified understanding was of an elevated romantic plaint. Such a pop gift served Whitfield and Strong well in another collaboration, the explicitly socially-aware "Ball of Confusion," a psychedelicized version of sixties protest anthems like Barry McGuire's "Eve of Destruction." Motown's Awareness phase could transcend trendiness with sheer oomph as "Ball of Confusion" proved, but "Smilin' Faces (Sometimes)" did it better by insinuating dis-ease.

No longer joyful, this Black protest admits a new element of pop paranoia that would lay in wait until rap. The pop world of 1971 didn't know what it was getting in "Smilin' Faces (Sometimes)"—bass notes and lowering tempos, with stark interjections piercing the strong male lead as the trio strains not to lose the murky melody. It's sinister sound mixed with Tupac's birth cries:

SMILIN' FACES (SOMETIMES)
PRETEND TO BE YOUR FRIEND
SMILIN' FACES
SHOW NO TRACES
OF THE EVIL THAT LURKS WITHIN

Whitfield's production anticipated the multilevel effects of hiphop. But even more, it gives a sensitive record of the breakdown in social confidence. Peace, Love, and Harmony are just in the singer's wishful imagination. Pain, Betrayal, and Disappointment are the harsh reality. The piquant female lines give a sexy aura—a sign that Black women feel this hurt, too; a suggestion that

Demonstration for the New York Panther 21.

Michael Abramson

the family, the community, is going through hell *together*, making this one of pop's most wised-up love songs—and one of the most bitter since those sung by Billie Holiday. Its splendid cynicism matches post-riot, post-CoIntelpro Black Panther Party outrage.

Afeni's involvement with the "New York 21" Panthers, accused of planning to bomb public spaces, was central to the party's eventual dissolution. (Imprisoned on more than 200 charges, she later defended herself successfully and was acquitted.) The party's splintered objectives over mission, strategy, and conduct dashed specific Black hopes for revolution *and* comradery. It was lyrically codified in a New York 21 letter sent to Panther headquarters in Oakland criticizing the party's West Coast branch of *"tripping out, pseudo-masochism, arrogance, myrmidonism, dogmatism, regionalism, regimentation, and fear. . ."* That letter proved somebody in the New York 21 had verbal skills and used them to express the same internal struggle between pretense and sincere despair that echoes in:

```
        The truth is in my eyes
        Cuz my eyes don't lie
                Amen
    Remember, a smile is just a frown
            Turned upside down
                My friend
```

That combination was both poignant and naive in those late-Panther days. In the late sixties and early seventies, Black youth was primed to act or comment on the need for social change. Student protest was a sign of this urge. The Student Non-violent Coordinating Committee (SNCC—a neo-logo/anagram worthy of rap's U.T.F.O. or Run-DMC) sought ways to express its acting-out, its activism, its bitterness, *and* its seriousness, by upping the stakes and sharpening the rhetoric of the civil rights movement. Free lunch programs to feed inner city children, who needed nourishment along with an improved educational structure, proved the intelligence and effectiveness of Panther activism. Restlessly progressive, eager to provoke change, SNCC brought an intensified purpose to the civil rights movement.

When its young leader, Stokely Carmichael, embraced Panther ideology, he demonstrated just the sort of drive and recklessness that defined the political yearning of enlightened Black youth. Carmichael's no-nonsense intensity, combined with the theatricality of Huey Newton's, Bobby Seale's, and Eldridge

Black Panthers in Central Park, New York City, at an Anti-Vietnam Demonstration, April 1969.

Claus C. Meyer

Cleaver's already histrionic Panthers, was inflammatory. Poised in a coordinated frieze of Black berets, leather, guns, and flags—a quasi-military parody of American male power—young Panthers were a definitive illustration of youth's infatuation with both force and change—the wild romance of independence. Sometimes uncontrollable, this spirit is distinguished by effrontery and nerve, the kind of daring that can bring down sensible strategies of resistance or foil plans for progress. This is what happened to 17-year-old Jonathan Jackson, young brother of Soledad prison Panther George Jackson. Jonathan, in a move as chaotic and slapstick-futile as a future rap video routine (e.g. Tupac's rolling with K-Ci and Danny Boy in *Toss It Up*), attempted to break George out of jail. Cut to the aftermath: George still behind bars and two cops dead, along with one young Panther—Jonathan.

Not just a casualty of "youth," this tragedy specifically illustrates the danger in unchecked zeal, the raging impatience Black youth are subject to in their wet, wild passion for creating justice—even, sometimes, through self-destructive backlash. This spark, recurring in Tupac's own wildness, determined the Panthers' apprehensive response to Jonathan Jackson's fiasco. Whether methodical or impulsive, rational or reactionary, the loss of faith after Jonathan's flashout singed the Panther's most instinctive connections. The party charred; optimism fell away before suspicion. Different styles of protest no longer coalesced: uniform principle dispersed in panic. Beset by outside investigations, East and West Coast rivalries posed young Black ambitions against each other. Every discordant note rankled.

More infamously catastrophic than Jonathan's teenage kamikaze act was the New York 21's controversial brush with celebrity. Panther party glamour—and the urgent correctness of its intensified civil rights push—captured the imaginations of white liberals whose support was catalogued and ridiculed by the imperiously indifferent Tom Wolfe in *Mau-Mauing the Flak-Catchers*.

A social group every bit as dreamy-eyed and susceptible as youth, white liberals ignored the complexities surrounding Panther activity. Acting on benevo-

Black Panthers in Central Park, New York City.

Shelley Rusten

ARMOND WHITE

lent impulses, they threw a party for the Panther 21's court defense. But, in addition to accruing Wolfe's snide distemper, the fundraiser also further estranged the East Coast Panthers from the original Oakland base. Across the nationhood of Black and White America, democracy was snapping and cracking as it went pop. Panthers who wanted social revolution now mixed it up with harsher radicals such as the Weathermen, extremists from the Students for a Democratic Society, whose anarchic tactics appealed to Panthers of a less tolerant, more impatient style. Passionate hubbub resulted and is perhaps best signified by a line Jane Fonda spoke at that Radical Chic gathering: "Revolution is an act of love. We are the children of revolution, born to be rebels—it runs in our blood." Proclaiming the Panthers "our revolutionary vanguard," she went on to declare: "We must support them with love, money, propaganda, and risk."

Only a churl—and a racist one at that—could laugh at Fonda's reasoning. While the future would embarrass her naivete, the contemporary moment certainly ennobled it. Romance was the irreducible element that kept Panther mystique going. Even if one extends the meaning of the word to include Afeni's personal affections, romance never is far off the mark when it comes to the political nature of peoples' lives. The intricacy of Afeni Shakur's love life—co-parenting with Billy Garland, co-habiting with Panther Lumumba Shakur, and later, with a mysterious drug dealer known as Legs—suggests a particular neo-democratic, libertarian turmoil. Afeni at the apex of a flesh-and-blood triangle, replicates the position of the female vocalist in The Undisputed Truth, who herself symbolizes the overstressed, ambivalent heart of Black America in the cloudy days after nonviolence and radicalism had both peaked.

Afeni Shakur's part in the New York 21 offers a young woman's version of Jonathan Jackson's impudence. While more personally, intimately contested, her desire and ambitions still reflect the sense of desperation that had overcome young adults who had seen so many of their ideals founder and dissipate. Afeni's choice of men, her commitment to fate, accident, whim, and dream are unextraordinary in the life of a contemporary woman and, therefore, part of the common human experience that bears the influence of fashion and principle as much as dream and depression. (Legs, the pusherman, propped her up when she couldn't stand on her own.) But Afeni—in love, lust, or principle—must have felt as Jane Fonda described, only, perhaps, with more commitment. As a member of the renegade New York 21, Afeni must also have conducted her romantic revolution with a degree of fuck-it-all radicalism. She empowered herself to make bold political and sexual decisions. Panther ideology in her head, Panther loyalty in her jail cell, Panther dialectic in her bed.

"Smilin' Faces (Sometimes)" dramatizes the duplicity that shocked the Panthers in their last days. Announcing the despair that would blanket Black America at the coming dawn of crack, the song makes real and sensual the spiritual drift that the militants had protested against. Listened to as serious gossip, it hints at deception and distrust. A shared ideology (a brother- and sisterhood) is being undermined in the song's "plot." As male voices control this narrative, the woman's voice shakes it. *The truth is in my eyes . . . Amen.* That's enough to dislodge any patriarchy's stability. Afeni's independence can be felt in that statement. Perfidious Eve is not the song's point; instead, the female singer subtly refuses the pressure put on her by men and circumstance. She'll give birth as her final judgment on the differences and disputes with which men, mostly, deceive.

Before rap with its harsh messages, it was impossible to imagine an R&B record with the pessimism of "Smilin' Faces (Sometimes)." (Backing vocals ask *"Can you dig it?"* preparing you for the worst that is to come. The lead male's moan, *"Oh, Lordy,"* is a vestige of the Negro spiritual—yesterday's protest genre now made to sound anachronistic.) It's realpolitik is not a matter of condemning society, but in the profound recognition of the failings humans are heir to. The warnings are blunt and emphatically repeated:

Beware!
Beware of the handshake
There hides a snake
Beware!
Beware of the pat on the back
It just might hold you back

It's that New York 21 letter made public, revealing to all the dissolution of comradery and hope. These are the passions—and confusions—Tupac was born into.

As a child of seventies pop, Tupac could bask in the Black consciousness that era's pop music made splendid—Curtis Mayfield's "Don't Worry," Marvin Gaye's "Mercy, Mercy Me (The Ecology)," Stevie Wonder's "You Haven't Done Nothin'," The Staple Singers' "Respect Yourself." If Afeni exposed her boy-child to such radio waves as "Smilin' Faces (Sometimes)," it had to be intended as an *unsentimental* education.[1] But the sentiment—an enthusiasm for Black intelligence, skepticism, and perseverance—still came through in pop's trenchant

[1]For herself, Afeni could sing Cheryl "Pepsii" Riley's "Thank you for my Child"(1989), one of he rare songs about single parenthood to address the mixed blessing of love-abandonment-redemption. It's a rarely delineated experience that, perhaps, required the hiphop era with its respect for the facts of life that had stigmatized the Black community, to ever be given full expression. Riley's song becomes Afeni's song because, in the lyrics of a single parent's self-realization, it makes a peace with the difficulty of a love relationship that doesn't last. There is forgiveness but also a stern determination to find a meaning in life—the sense to make joy and substance out of the fleeting pleasure and eventual hurt of a human liaison.

While Afeni might not quite agree with Riley's second layer of meaning that turns a mother's resignation into holy devotion—it might seem too conventional—there is, yet, sentimental certainty that Afeni, the Black American woman radical who was principled, and traditional enough to avail herself of membership in Rev. Herbert Daughtry's The House of the Lord Church, relates quite passionately to Riley's praise to God. The politically conscious woman and the love-conscious young girl share the hope that a parent places in the life of a child, a hope for future companionship, for a continuation of her own line of belief and heritage.

swing: the flow and embrace of the music, the active, rebellious potential in dancing, head-bobbing, finger-snapping.

In this way, ideas that represented the evolution of Black political protest and social enterprise became an unmistakable part of that era's popular currency. Revolt was absorbed by young minds as naturally as if it were a given of Black living habits. Spike Lee missed this insight in *Crooklyn*'s story of seventies hellions, ignoring the part culture played in the formative years of his generation, and how he, his siblings, and contemporaries processed the images and ideas of pop's radical gestalt. What Lee, and perhaps other seventies teens, took for granted, Tupac's succeeding generation saw as their legacy. Lee's generation had seen just enough of the civil rights movement's tumultuous striving—the despondency of mid-sixties riots, the shock of the decade's assassinations, and the splintering of youthful outrage into various, bold, scarey groups—to know what sacrifices were at stake in the Black struggle. Tupac's generation had no sense of the stake, only an awareness that some sacrifice was still being exacted—unfairly.

This corresponds to the devastating fact of homelessness: the experience of sacrifice without a justifying purpose. Poverty and social disruption became the terms of Tupac's youth, which the exuberance of seventies pop contrasted not quite mockingly, but sardonically. By the time Tupac was five, his life began to mirror pop's heightened big-screen versions. Mama Afeni—her words vocalized by Gladys Knight, her avidity portrayed by Diahann Carroll in the movie *Claudine*—lived a life that delineated the funhouse distortion of great ideas into grim truth. For a kid raised on pop, this could only result in confusion, intensified by the frustration teens feel at life's inability to imitate media fantasy. For Tupac, the conditions of poverty were surreal because their cause seemed incomprehensible and impervious to change. This would directly influence the aesthetic of Tupac's raps.

Living in a psychosocial limbo, Tupac tangled with the meanings of rootlessness as his mother moved house: from the Bronx to Brooklyn, from apartments to shelters, from city to city. Hints of motivation came through in the decisions to migrate—the packing-up of troubles and the relocation of opportunity. But without understanding, a mobile child can only manufacture sense by developing

a compensatory, defensive sensibility. Tupac's was based on the one thing he was sure of—that no home, no community, no goal was certain.

His childhood in New York was shadowed by the failure of the dissolute Panthers. Along with the party's collapse, the taut communal spirit that believed in an improving change had evaporated. Lack of opportunity underscores this desolation; its effect on the morale of parents and neighbors seeps into a child's innocence and kills it. The support system that insures a child's spiritual growth is attenuated, in spite of Afeni's best intentions to encourage and protect it.

Only naturally, the child's resilient mind rallied. Family acquaintances describe Tupac's shyness—a certain sign of active fantasy life, making up for the father-son interaction he longed for but lacked. A classmate reports on Tupac's artistic interests: "He wrote some poetry to me then. He was sincere, very sincere."

While not the average boy-boy activity (until rap), poetry-writing suggests a mind above street level. (It was punk-infatuated Chryssie Hynde who, in "Message of Love," quoted Oscar Wilde: *"We are all of us in the gutter/ Some of us are looking at the stars.")* Poetry's ordering of words and feeling expresses a desire to remake the commonplace into an example of its transcendence. Even trite poetry—perhaps *especially* trite poetry—expresses a hunger for sublimity. It would be easy to say that Tupac found his inspiration in then-prevalent examples of rap DJing—the advent of Funky Four Plus One, the Treacherous Three, and Sugarhill Gang made an impact, no doubt. But at ten, Tupac's impulse to write and share poetry more impressively expresses a solitaire's motivation that is psyche-deep, not fashion-slick.

Was this a grounding? Perhaps not ideal, but it's what Tupac had as he set out to make his own lifestory in hiphop. And it explains the complicated interweave of angry suppositions, desperate rationalizations, and entrancing emotional flow that ruled his life as it shaped his lyrical content.

Press "Play" on Tupac's 1996 recording, "I Ain't Mad at Cha," and you can hear echoes of "Smilin' Faces (Sometimes)"—not in an actual musical sample, but in the suggestions of menace and distrust cutting through the urban folksiness. This is the piquant, naive combination of theatricality and lost hope as a nineties artist would convey it. He's cut off from the roots of dislocation that inspired The Undisputed Truth, yet intent on making vivid a half-truth about the conditions of contemporary Black survival—Tupac's own—in his ambivalent oration that mixes fun with anger and despair. Afeni's generation possessed social insight too penetrating to tolerate such ambivalence even as a guileful dramatic stance. For Tupac, the stance was what most remained from that era's turmoil. His artistic sensibility compelled him to affect a modern posture. Revolution's love-child, Tupac gravitated toward using the slings and arrows of racist America's outrageous fortune.

Hit "Play" again: See Tupac as a quasi-political cupid, armed with the bluff and ardor of a generation that means to do things differently, advancing on the world's stage. He's born shrewd—yet innocent.

CHAPTER 3
east vs. waste

"gotta stay swift," a West Coast acquaintance remembers Tupac saying whenever he talked about his family's constant movement, partly to show off his street smarts, partly in self-defense. Tupac never had a chance to graduate from the Baltimore School of the Arts. He was seventeen when Afeni, in flight from the troubles that had led her into crack addiction, moved her family to Marin City, on the West Coast. Tupac, who might have been dreaming of the green, grassy amenities of a California suburb, found himself a continent away from "home," stranded in yet another bleak, burned-out, drug-swamped urban ghetto. "Leaving BSA affected me so much," Tupac said later, with real sorrow. "I see that as the point where I got off the track . . ."Although for a time, Tupac attended Tamalpais High School, he didn't stay there long enough to graduate and later received a general equivalency diploma.

Those first years of Tupac's Northern California sojourn came down to scrounging for a living, hustling, selling drugs—even fighting with Afeni. Tupac watched a frightening cloud of despair settle over his mother—the same mood of desolation that seemed to be suffocating the West Coast community he was just discovering. As the only male in the household, driven by an itching aspiration toward manhood, Tupac was in turmoil. It wasn't long before he left home to move in with a new friend in the neighborhood. According to Rev. Daughtry, "They said he hit bottom. He was constantly looking for a place to stay and something to eat. It seemed nobody liked him in those days, except his mother . . ."

This breakout west could be thought of as a typical on-the-road youthful exploration—what's generally depicted as a white myth—but as it happens, Black American youth dealing with the same disorientation, feeling the same need to embark on a spiritual quest, also forges its own road mythology.

Staying swift, Tupac began a moral juggling act; he sold drugs and wrote poetry. With visions of L.L.Cool J. still in his head, Tupac saw in hiphop his dream of personal salvation. Leila Steinberg, the retired dancer and singer from Sonoma County who eventually became Tupac's first manager, recalled their first meeting:

> **He had a real difficult living situation in Marin City and I always had the household that anybody that needed a spot or whatever, came through. And so, I was [teaching arts in local school] programs, and 'Pac did some of his poetry and rapped for me. And I thought he was probably the most brilliant young poet, rapper, whatever, I'd ever heard.**

Tupac circled around Marin City rap culture seeking a resolution to his rootlessness. Ray Luv was another ambitious young man working with Steinberg. Soon Tupac and Luv were part of the short-lived six-member group, Strictly Dope, performing at local clubs and house parties, struggling to produce a demo that could lead to a record deal. When they announced plans to go professional,

Tupac and Luv turned to Steinberg, asking her to manage them. Not feeling up to it, she turned them down. "Well, you're gonna," Tupac insisted. "I already see it. You would be the best manager." And he was right. It was Steinberg who introduced Tupac and Ray Luv to her friend Atron Gregory, who had started his own record label, TNT, featuring a local rap group, Digital Underground.

"I had a party at my house," Steinberg recalls. "And I made a video. . . It was like the video of the artists I finally decided I was going to represent. So I made this video and sent it to Atron. And he said "I don't know, You have to take them to Shock G from Digital, and he'll tell me if he thinks Tupac's that tight."

But Strictly Dope wasn't working out. Ray Luv's father didn't want him to continue with the group, so Steinberg drove Tupac to Starlight Studios to meet Digital's leader, Greg Jacobs (Shock G). "I said, 'Greg, you know, I've got this artist and you gotta hear him 'cause I want Atron to give us a record deal." After spending a year trying to convince Bay Area music dreamers to bet on Tupac, Steinberg finally got an audience. "Tupac floored Greg. Completely. He was so tight." Steinberg begged Greg Jacobs to let Tupac work with Digital. "And that's how it got started."

With this new impetus, Tupac hooked up again with Ray Luv and Strictly Dope had a brief resurgence. It lasted long enough for the duo to sign up with TNT and record some tracks under Greg Jacobs' supervision. "That whole album is finished," says Steinberg. "That's an album that's never been released. It's Tupac's first album, as a member of Strictly Dope. Atron owns the masters and holds the rights to the first album. Maybe one day he'll put it out."

Luv's father finally persuaded his son to quit. With his showbiz prospects back on the shelf, Tupac's thoughts turned to education. "I used to pull 'Pac in, I would have him help do my work in schools," Steinberg told *4080* magazine. "He always had this commitment to education. And I was working on curriculums. I always felt that if the curriculums were different and people of color were represented in schools, all people of all colors, then we'd have a different society. And he always supported that."

In limbo again, Tupac considered a move to Atlanta as part of a student organization. His curiosity and restlessness had a political aspect, too. In 1989, Tupac became chairman of a group called the New African Panthers, young brothers determined to honor the goals of the original party without repeating its mistakes. *Rap Sheet* magazine reported on this adventure as a brief respite from the Marin City rap race. New African Panthers' out-of-town location put Tupac on the road for a month as their youngest-ever chairman.

But Tupac would trade New African Panther social activism for another sort of activism that, at least in its flash and novelty, seemed to strike more sparks in the imaginations of young Black brothers. There was also the promise of fun. Instead of underground political activity, Tupac was bedazzled by a new approach that parodied revolution through the subversiveness of pleasure. This was personified by Digital Underground. Stressing the oldest meaning of the word "party," wearing freakazoid disguises to accent the purely libidinal aspects of Black pop, the Bay Area rap group played on the decade's infatuation with hiphop, reviving dance music in newer, wilder styles. Their only big hit, "The Humpty Dance" was a neo-pornographic mix of eighties funk (like Cameo's "Word Up") and sexual compulsion (put in comical code by George Clinton's "Atomic Dog"), made acceptably licentious (by the Prince of *Dirty Mind*).

The group's name suggested a computer-age manifestation of gut-bucket secrets. Shock G, Digital Underground's lead vocalist, assumed a second role as Humpty Hump, a commedia dell'arte figure with an exaggerated, phallic nose and a distorted, nasal vocal delivery meant to sound as if he were rapping from under the sheets.

Before the "The Humpty Dance," rap had few actual dance cuts—Rob Base and DJ Easy Rock's sublime "It Takes Two" was a rare hit, derived from the incessant momentum of club music. "The Humpty Dance" retained rap's percussive speaking rhythms, translating the dance/party ethic to hiphop.

Digital Underground's energy level struck a chord with Tupac, who auditioned to join the group. His association with Greg Jacobs and Digital's other founding member, Money B, formed a bond of ambition and like mindedness that was impossible to shake off. In 1990, Shock G took him on; first, as a roadie; then as a dancer. Steinberg says:

Greg asked 'Pac to come on the road with him and be a dancer. And the thing was 'Pac was always an artist in his own right. And the funny thing is, he may have been a background dancer for Digital underground, but I swear to God he took the stage every time. He could've been a background person, [still] he out-shined everybody on every stage he was ever on. That's real.

The leading rap groups were developing new styles of stage presentation. Dancers now had a fundamental role in supplying the visual excitement that rappers themselves rarely provided as they marched back and forth along the edge of the stage. At BSA, Tupac had trained in ballet, acquiring a discipline that refined his agility and focused his physical energy. The early nineties offered a rare opportunity for Black males to take the eye-candy spotlight usually reserved for women. Suddenly, young men were displaying a different kind of athleticism—not dreaming of Michael Jackson/James Brown glory, but dancing out the steps and body twists that came straight from the streets. It wouldn't be long before Oakland's MC Hammer rode that style straight to a stardom that represented a cultural ethos. (One of John Singleton's first films, *Steppin into the House,* featured overlapping low-rent images of the dance-rap group 06 Style showing off their choreographic charms.) Tupac fell into the dance spell for Digital Underground, but dance was never enough. It was through his appearance on their *This is an EP* "Same Song" video in 1991, that Tupac first realized the thrill of putting a rhyme on tape and getting it to the public.

Digital Underground in 1990 (Tupac Shakur is on the left).

Raymond Boyd/Michael Ochs Archive

Digital Underground offered platinum promise along with a considerable fun quotient. The names of the group's production company, "Stayin' Busy," and their writing collective, "Underground Write-How-You-Like Regime," (playing off "The Humpty Dance" code words "Do what you like") flaunted their flippancy. These jokers could easily waylay a young warrior's more serious intentions—or at least complicate them.

On "Same Song" samples "Theme to the Black Hole" by Parliament, Digital Underground prescribes dancing as a response to the world's dulling repetition and the ghetto's grim lack of opportunity. But when Tupac joins the fun with his first mainstream rap, his smile turns into a frown:

**PEOPLE CHANGE
WANT TO LIVE THEY LIFE HIGH
SAME SONG
CAN'T GO WRONG
IF I PLAY THE NICE GUY**

Humpty interjects: *"Claim to fame/ Must be changed/ Now that we became strong."*

This track presents Tupac as a highly self-conscious, nineties' Candide. "Same Song's" chorus chants "Been all around the world," bringing DJ Quik's worldly realization into Tupac's sense of the world and suggesting that the fickleness of rap's social action already bores him. His awareness of public jealousy is already more substantive than Digital Underground's usual subjects. Instead of not minding how he's seen (like Shock G), Tupac is all too aware of how he comes off, upsetting people with his outsized ambition, his drive to achieve. For his professional debut, Tupac has traveled from the troubled but principled East to the pleasure-struck West where showbiz, or non-activism—what Afeni might consider waste—has zonked him with the lure of its complex rewards. The line "If I play the nice guy" will become the subtext of everything else he ever records. Hiphop's Candide faces the first of many moral lessons and political crises.

If it hadn't been for a minor police incident, 1991 might have been remembered as the year of Tupac's clear, hopeful send off, but when he was stopped by police in downtown Oakland and cited for jaywalking, his East/ West journey was suddenly clouded by omens of trouble to come.

Afeni sensed this happening. She had become an interested observer of hiphop, taking notice whenever there was a record that took into account the complications Black America was going through. At the time of Tupac's first record success, she took note of "a song that says something. I hear some of Tupac's stories in it." The reference is to DJ Quik's "Jus Lyke Compton," a road song that came from the new generation of rappers but also meant something to an ex-Panther who had led the life of a road-running fugitive. *"Finally left the motherfuckin' C-P-T/ Off to other cities and shit/ No longer just an underground hit/ Movin' things/ A local nigga made good/ And made a name offa makin' tapes for niggas in the 'hood/ Let me tell a little story/ about the places that I been to/ And the shit that I been through."*

While the romance of the road suffuses this song, Quik's narration gets swiftly to the sobering reality of career-sanctioned "freedom"—the lateral social movement that undermines the dream of showbiz success. *"Foolish was I to think there wasn't other cities like this/ And they didn't like this,"* he reasons. Any American traveling across the continent, seeing the poverty and squalor common to the life of our national underclass, knows this let down, and Tupac on the road felt no differently. "Quik got it right," he said, while in the studio making *Strictly For My N.I.G.G.A.Z.*, Quik's tune accounts for the disillusionment awaiting naive, would-be rappers who, like Tupac, thought themselves on the road to an All-American Oz. *"That's when I started thinking this wasn't like home/ But then they had to prove me wrong."*

"Now Oakland is just like Compton," Quick begins and now the song sounds prophetic to Tupac, who had come from the bright promise of BSA to the ruins of Oakland. Spooky fate laughs in the background of Quik's odyssey, a ghostly chorus. From Oakland to St. Louis, San Antonio to Denver, Quik

observes: *"How could a bunch of niggas in a town like this/ Have such a big influence on niggas so far away?"* Once in Marin City, Tupac took up Quik's wondering about hiphop's expansion. The song spoke to the spread of social disaster Tupac saw wherever he went, to the longed-for radical changes that neither he nor Afeni could find anywhere. Its sense of an elusive homeland made music of the discomfort they experienced first hand. (An experience from which political commentators are so remote—they lack either personal knowledge or the simple curiosity to set it out or address it.) But the delight of this song is that—in the joy and ingenuity of Quik's rhymes, illustrative observations, humorous details, and clever asides—it creates its own place of intellectual and moral stability in the art of hiphop, in the very act of rapping.

This is what Tupac meant by describing rap as "this new thing that had no boundaries and was so different to everyday music." It offered an alternative way of coping. In hiphop was a philosophy reborn from what Afeni knew and central to the way Tupac's generation saw the world, particularly how he viewed the late-eighties ruins of Oakland—a stark contrast to Panther dreams.

Recovering from the burned-out pipe dreams of a fallen Bay Area, Afeni remained intelligent and articulate. Described as "one of the most powerful spokespersons" of the activist movement in the late sixties and early seventies, no one who knew her at that time could have guessed that she would fall victim to drugs and all the terrifying things that go with it. Afeni had faced down the government, she had campaigned for improvement, raised two kids, bounced from ghetto to town to coast.

A friend sympathized with Afeni's breakdown, "Like a lot of women who struggle with a bad situation, I also used. I didn't tell anybody, including my family. I just hid in my little world of drugs." The intention was to block out the contradiction between drug use and political views. Afeni would prefer rap creativity to be her son's sinecure, even while she sought to relieve the letdown of failed activism through abuse. The Bay Area had become an arena of waste; its streets and houses, its forgotten history, all exemplified how a lot of people who had once seen liberty in "the movement" now sought uneasy escape from despair in drugs. "There were a lot of stressful and disappointing things happening," former activist Valerie McFall, who had helped organize Jonathan Jackson's Soledad assault, explained. "A lot of the things we tried to do, we didn't. We failed at it and that's hard to accept."

But in 1991, Tupac's response was to accept his own generation's alternative to sixties radicalism: in rap he found a sense of promise.

CHAPTER 4
the b-boy bounce

"America's Nightmare: Mutulu Shakur,
Assata Shakur"

—Tupac on "Wordz of Wisdom"

how many shakurs does it take
to raise a child, an artist, a revolutionary? The home environment Afeni provided might have been short on material comforts but it did ensure—for a time, anyway—the presence of progressive examples for her children,

Afeni had not disclosed the identity of Tupac's father but she made it clear that it was not Lumumba Shakur, who was the lead defendant in the Panther 21 case, her husband at the time of the trial and through her pregnancy. Soon after, acquitted and released from jail, Afeni moved in with Lumumba's adopted brother, Mutulu. Mutulu Shakur (born Jeral Wayne Williams)—the father of Tupac's brother, Mopreme—was not a mere figurehead but a model of radicalism for the family to emulate.

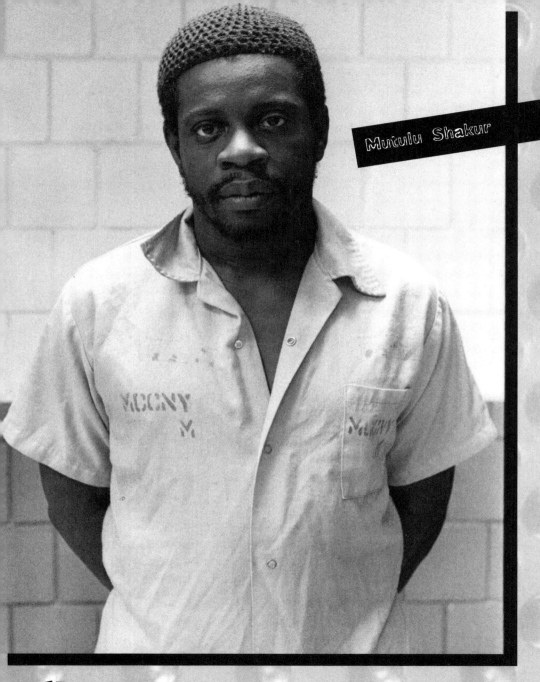

Mutulu Shakur

ARMOND WHITE

But, fleeing her own demons, Afeni would move her children West before Tupac was seventeen and before he could graduate from the Baltimore School of the Arts. Afeni's ambitious, idealized family plan was doomed by poverty and discouragement; the domestic conventions that she had so fiercely opposed would backfire disastrously. A dire irony: Family was the only means to self-sufficiency but also, inadvertently, a trap. Caught between poverty and the implicit luxury of radicalism, there wasn't adequate support from society at large or from her personal network to realize the familial transformation she had once so passionately envisioned.

Convicted for his involvement in the infamous 1981 armored car robbery that left two Nyack, N.Y., policemen and a Brinks guard dead, Mutulu still claimed his innocence. Taken away from the family circle, he continued to think of himself as a help-mate to the family. "Father, friend, comrade" is how he described his relationship to Tupac. Conversations between them were, as Tupac poignantly remembered, "good lessons." Histories, examples, anecdotes were passed along. "He taught me important things about loyalty, about fighting, about beliefs. All the stuff a young nigga need to know not to fall for the shit waitin' out here. Just us two, talkin'." And relating. Until the law intervened, forcing the growing boy and embattled man to face the disruption of trust, compassion, and loyalty implicit in the bond of "father, friend, comrade." Following Mutulu's incarceration, this private tragedy fanned outward.

Shakur, Shakur, Shakur. Said aloud, the name suggests a litany of cultural ambition, the coming together of heroic beliefs in an extended family, a nuclear community. But dispersal and doom broke the circle. Lumumba was found murdered in Louisiana just before Mutulu's arrest. Assata Shakur, the woman most often confused with Afeni in the mainstream media, was born Joanne Chesimard. She gained prominence in 1973, when she and Zayd Shakur, brother to Mutulu and Lumumba, were stopped by a New Jersey state trooper. In the shootout that followed, Zayd and Trooper Werner Foerster were killed; Assata was wounded and later convicted. Representing an extreme case of Black activism, federal authorities said Mutulu had helped Assata escape from prison in 1979, when she became aware of a plan to assassinate her. Securing her own legend, Assata fled to Cuba where she currently lives under asylum granted by Fidel Castro.

The Shakurs' tribal activism had become both a legend and a legacy. Journalist Ron Howell reported: "At fifteen, Tupac must have been thoroughly convinced that to be a Shakur was to confront the possibility of death at an early age. He was learning such lessons almost before he could walk."

In the British magazine *The Face*, David Toop, reflecting on Tupac's upbringing, observed: "Tupac's family history is convoluted hearsay, but a number of prominent Panthers, including Geronimo Pratt and Mutulu Shakur, figured in his early life. Unsurprisingly, Tupac appears to have been torn in half: family connections and his sympathies for the Panthers' revolutionary action on one side; the material world and its pleasures on the other."

The Source magazine, reporting on one of Tupac's trials, mentioned the support of Attorney Chokwe Lumumba, National Chairman of the Revolutionary New Afrikan People's Organization, acting as Tupac's legal advisor. An ex-Panther, Lumumba took the stand and testified to Tupac's "ambition, his productiveness, and his desire to be useful to his community."

Not too many months later, on the night of Tupac's death, Mutulu would muse: "You pushed so many away. You burnt so many bridges so they wouldn't follow you into battles against the demons you were facing. Knowing well to what lengths you would go. This battlefield of reality is littered with many meaningless casualties." That's father speaking to son one last time, across a chasm more unbridgeable than the generation gap.

Tupac, a baby of the Black Power movement, would never attain the distance or perspective necessary to critique the ideas he was taught. Instead, he'd be bound to them—ambivalently, of course—through affection. Like Afeni, he would feel the necessity to achieve some kind of rapprochement with African heritage. But all he had was rap's beat to take with him as he embarked on his quest.

During the 1992 filming of John Singleton's movie, *Poetic Justice*, Tupac told Veronica Chambers how he felt the world must regard him: "You've never seen a young black male grow up, but now you have to watch, and you have to help, because my father is not alive. This system took him, so it's up to everybody else to raise me." Recounting that quote in *Esquire Magazine*, Chambers lets it stand on its own, supporting Tupac's self-mythologizing. At that time he had not yet met his biological father, Billy Garland. For Chambers, Tupac put on the same act he did for others, fantasizing the incarcerated Lumumba Abdul Shakur as his father. Like Frankie in Carson McCullers' novel of teen isolation and longing, *Member of the Wedding*, Tupac got a sense of wholeness by projecting onto Lumumba and Afeni "the we of me."

Tupac envied Singleton's stable family. "John had a father that cared, but I didn't have one," he told a reporter, who noted his voice became thick with longing. "Singleton knew that part of my pain, because he knew how hard it is to grow up without [a father]." Given the sadness of such an emotional state, hiphop fans and reporters indulged much of Tupac's self-pity. Yet, referring to Mutulu's conviction, Tupac told a hiphop convention: "I know a warrior, y'all, you don't take no bullshit, no crying about my mama couldn't, my daddy didn't stay. He stood up for his own self," and that speech won over a crowd thrilled to see a young Black man take responsibility for himself. It contradicted the lost-father sentiment that had already become a hiphop cliche.

In "Wordz of Wisdom," Tupac buckjumped over his depression to achieve communion with the people and beliefs he felt were his inheritance. His search is apparent in the soundtrack, too—laid-back yet steady, depicting a subtle assertiveness.

"Wordz of Wisdom displays a political and an artistic inheritance. Gil Scott-Heron was part of the cultural indoctrination that was mother's milk to Tupac's generation. Scott-Heron's knack for polemical poetry recited to a jazz-funk band struck an ideological chord. It represented a new gesture of relevance that young folks could groove to and call their own style—a presentiment of rap's own reclamation of the beat. Think of Scott-Heron's music as a parallel soundtrack to the fantasies being ground out by Blaxploitation movies; this was the seventies soundtrack enlightened young Blacks preferred. Scott-Heron's new style charted the changes in progressive Black rhetoric in the very cover art of his 1975 release, *The First Minute of a New Day*, that renders the famous Huey Newton pose in the wicker fan chair as a cartoon with a guerilla in the catbird seat. (George Clinton would later parody the pose to more popular acclaim but less political meaning on *Uncle Jam Wants You*.) A lite-funk groove, the track "Guerilla" suggested a becalmed revolution—pop resistance through the most restrained and sedate body movement. According to Tupac, Mutulu "liked that 'Revolution Will Not Be Televized' rap." Scott-Heron's fusion pushed, its effect came more from earnestness than musicality. *"Trying to get someplace in the human race/ 'Cause we need to see black babies smile,"* he chants on "Guerilla." And his reference point is Tupac's generation.

'I'm going through the same shit that my daddy went through When he was 22 Now who's The hell to blame?'

"All the heroes done been killed or sent away/ The people know it's winter in America/ And ain't nobody fighting/ 'Cause nobody knows what to say." Scott-Heron's seriousness, his griot-like doling out of common sense prophecy, moved listeners. Tupac had been raised during that "winter in America." Such Scott-Heron lines as "America leads the world in shocks . . . the poor go to jail while the rich go to San Clemente" (from "Pardon Our Analysis") make specific charges, fueling the political indignation Mutulu would impart to Tupac and

thus forging the backdrop for the indignation one finds in a Tupac lyric. Together, Tupac and Mutulu, who stayed in contact by phone, drew up a "Code of Thug Life," listing rules of behavior to discourage gangsta rappers from violence.

The seventies habit of analyzing contemporary politics and reacting to it on record is replaced, in the nineties, by an internalized disgust with the surrounding world. This is a backtracking, a rewind of political consciousness to a time even before Scott-Heron's generation—a time when the sources of Black despair could not even be named. While Tupac took passion from his elders, his blind lashing out rebelled against the intellectual diatribes that characterized the pride and political trusts of the failed SNCC-Panther-campus-upstarts.

This, too, is what is meant by the popular hiphop phrase "ghetto bastard." It's a grief that cuts two ways, a feeling of abandonment that swallows up both parent and child. For Mutulu to be locked up out of reach, and Geronimo Pratt, Tupac's godfather and another convicted Black Panther, also unavailable for daily counseling, means shared feelings of oppression and desires for retaliation were not communicated but lost in each man's bewilderment at the overwhelming circumstances that engulfed him. Tupac would admire how succinctly Scarface expressed it in "Point of No Return": *I'm going through/ the same shit that my daddy went through/ When he was 22/ Now who's/ The hell to blame?"*

Tupac understood how ghetto bastards felt bereft of guidance because he saw evidence of it all around him—especially in the Bay Area's new generation of desperate young Black men. Tupac shook his head for a TV interviewer and wondered. "I don't know why the message got lost." It was a typical rap-era statement, referring to how American pop, including hiphop jumbles messages in a flux of ideas whether shiny and new or golden oldie. But it's understandable how hiphoppers got sideswiped by the thrill of celebration that had fooled them all into thinking their particular experience was different from that of their forefathers. The flattery of Big New Thing promotion and the inherent puffery of the teenage exploitation business can split artists off from their heritage.

Playing this role, Tupac complained to MTV: "All the society is doin' is leechin' off the ghetto; they use the ghetto for their pain, for their sorrow, for their culture, for their music, for their happiness, for their movies." That's youthful vanity talking, the force of what some people have called "ghettocentricity"—a delusion that traps hiphop youth in their own achievements. Tupac was high on the media's worship and corruption of Black youth yet, at the same time, contemptuous. It takes a particular insight to see past this cultural inversion.

After Lou Reed's notorious 1978 "I Wanna be Black"—a racist summation of the White Negro fascination that persists in both bohemian and leftist sympathies—he made a good, underrated album that applied American rock star experience to the adolescent questioning then fashionable in British punk rock circles. *Growing Up in Public* (1980) stands as a curious document, pertinent to the barely understood maturation process that would become an issue for emerging hiphoppers. Reed's timely personal assessment of the masculinity he was brutishly taught and that he awkwardly strove to personify, clarified a psychosocial dilemma that rock—the music of a pampered generation—could not fully explore until rap grew into that subject almost haphazardly. It was a part of the masculine pressure inherited by young Black men and by Black male artists through the geneology of late-seventies songs like "Papa Was a Rolling Stone" and "Patches."

Reed rapped: *"They edify your integrity so they can play on your fears/ And they're gonna do it public /Cuz you're growin' up in public/ Growing up in public with your pants down."* Matching the tough street sense of Kurtis Blow's "The Breaks," here is the process of commercial exploitation stated directly and tied to the not-disinterested goal of the naive artist who, like Tupac, longed for both success and exposure.

As Tupac told the media about his need to fight for his freedom of expression as a rap performer, Reed's album became a cautionary tale for a young artist. Tupac realized that the music industry's access to the public's attention gave him the voice his people had dreamed of for generations—a rare opportunity to tell the truth, to make a difference. When Reed made an allegory of this circumstance with an updated classical reference—*"Prince Hamlet caught in the middle between reason and instinct/ Caught in the middle with his pants down again"*—his own pop-professional experience gives him the insight Kurtis Blow was only just coming to.

The Hamlet line is so close to what rappers contend with in their effort to move through life and showbiz with strength and honor that Shakespeare's dramatized mixup of masculinity and honor is relevant to Black artists in their contemporary struggle for both honor (reason) and independence (instinct). Tupac represents the Prince Hamlets of hiphop, scions of revolution caught between industry exploitation and their own political demands. But like Hamlet, haunted by a missing father, driven by hysterical principles, these princely rappers are often caught with their pants down—showing their asses and exposing an intellectual vulnerability that results from a deep desire to right long-standing offenses, even if only in the grooves of their own recordings.

Reed's records were among those Tupac was known to listen to slyly, in his private collection, and when cruising in his own car. Enjoying the Bay Area's polyglot culture and the range of influences gained from his scattered education, a whole host of white artists found their way onto Tupac's playlist: Sinead O'Connor, U2, Culture Club. Lamping among the party-hearty eclecticism of Digital Underground, Tupac took on the nickname, Rebel of the Underground—a reference to his Panther background, but also to his own unique way of doing things. "We'd be tripping to Neneh Cherry's 'Buffalo Stance,'" a friend remembers from those early Bay Area days, "and 'Pac would follow that shit up with some Pet Shop Boys, 'Left to My Own Devices' and then back that up with 'My Prerogative' by Bobby Brown. Some Bobby Womack shit be in there, too. He was like some kind of underground DJ, doing dope mixes in his head."

When a journalist brought Cecil and Linda Womack's *Transformation to the House of Zekkariyas* to Tupac's attention, he enthusiastically shot back,

"That sounds like some dope shit. Where can I hear that?" Not a rap album, *Transformation* exists only because of the changed climate in Black cultural thought that hiphop had created. R&B masters, Womack and Womack took advantage of Black pop's new youthful emphasis by encouraging their children to join in the creation and production of the record. They went so far into a personal version of Afrocentricity that they left the pop and hiphop bazaar behind them. Hard-hearted Makaveli might have been rejuvenated by it.

An R&B album evincing the virtues of family togetherness seemed out of sync with the Black self-destruction that fascinated the early-nineties marketplace—even though it might have been recognized as a fortunate consequence of Arrested Development's back-to-their roots popularity. But these actually were signs of a scrupulous attempt at catching the energy and integrity of the hiphop era—a work of Afro-eccentricity. This doesn't mean simply wearing tribal clothes amd spouting Kwanzaa homilies—the guise of many narrowminded Black folks. *Transformation* peculiarly but sensibly gets in the nap and wrinkle of family life.

Perhaps *Transformation* simply stunned the pop industry through its extraordinary, unexpected wisdom. Reviewing their own marriage for the complexities that trouble any mature couple impelled Linda and Cecil Womack to a new consideration of their roots. After visiting Nigeria, they took on the name Zekkariyas "in honor of their original and true identity." The transforming act itself is full of faith. *Transformation to the House of Zekkariyas* means to revitalize R&B, if not through innovation, then by confirming its pertinence to Black life experience.

The album began with Cecil and Linda—Zekkariyas and Zeriiya—transforming songs composed by their teenaged daughters, Zeniya and Zekuumba. It's a family endeavor yet doesn't stray from the Womack and Womack niche where romantic complications provoke lots of feeling and wise reflection. The adult knowledge in these songs goes beyond the scope of teenage understanding, and when some of the lyrics strain toward callowness, the maturity of the parents' vocals carries the songs with power and style. The Womacks get past superficial styles and achieve the dream of Family Afrocentricity.

In the period that intervenes between Tupac's birth, the death of the Panthers, and the age of newly created Black wealth in Reagan's America, something vague yet momentous happened, affecting the poignancy of the parent-to-child, find-your-roots ambition. In the Eighties, as the Horatio Alger myth was literalized—deepened—into a tenet of Black social beliefs, the greedily bourgeois *Putney Swope* ideal came into being. It took many years, many generations of middle-class Blacks struggling to fit in with the typical American plan before waking up and finding a better way. Those years absorbed the fascination with genealogy that began with Alex Haley's *Roots,* and then saw that ethnocentricity wane or settle into the more conventional practice of Kwanzaa. The Black struggle for a dream would have to overcome the middle-class drive for status and force family and heritage to come together as a spiritual goal. Afeni tried pulling this off. She had begun by giving her children Afrocentric names that attested to standards of Black independence and heritage that took precedence over notions of propriety held by previous generations that prized Western assimilation. But with Mutulu gone and crack, her East Coast adversary, seeping into the Bay Area Black community, it was a great deal more than Afeni could pull off by herself.

In 1990, on tour with Digital Underground, Tupac discovered Afeni had succumbed to drugs again. "Here we was kickin' all this shit about the revolution—and we starvin," Tupac said. "That didn't make no sense to me."

CHAPTER 5
children will listen

2pacalypse now, Tupac's debut album, revealed cultural indebtedness with almost disarming naivete. In retrospect, the sound of Tupac first, developing social views and artistic voice, has untold promise. Writing and recording this album was his artistic answer to the political principles taught by Afeni and Mutulu, Rev. Daughtry, and Public Enemy—his elders, who held in common with the Zekkariyases a hopeful parental wisdom expressed in a song by Stephen Sondheim in "Children Will Listen."

> How do you say to your child in the night
> 'Nothing's all black but then nothing's all white?'
> How do you say it will all be alright/
> When you know that it mightn't be true?
> What do you do?

Black parents worry so much, carefully weighing the correct amounts of morality to dispense against the very real injustices of daily living—and wait to see those lessons heeded. Afeni's need to prepare her child for his own protection, for his own need for revolution, reached deeply into what she believed to be sensible and what she believed to be necessary. For Tupac's guardians , broken and struggling anew, heritage wasn't the certainty it seemed for the Zekkariyases. History bore down upon each of Afeni's lessons and Mutulu's reprimands.

```
What do you leave to your child when you're dead?
        Only whatever you put in its head
    Things that your mother and father had said
           that were left to them too . . .
```

Written by Stephen Sondheim for his musical, *Into the Woods*, "Children Will Listen" cautions about the lessons inherent in parental instruction, in the way children are initiated into ideology, guided through various mythologies, whether political, psychological, or sexual. These mythologies are handed down through folk lore—the kind the Zekkariyas parents, in the nineties, knew to make available to their children, inviting them to take part in creating—and, thus, in understanding and control.

For young Black families of the seventies, much of that lore was found in the proto-rap expressions of The Last Poets and Gil Scott-Heron. These spiritual fathers took the place of the lost male figures Tupac lamented. Loneliness encouraged his infatuation with a Bad Father—Legs, the drug dealer, who introduced Afeni to crack. Misguided, Tupac still drew from Legs' example of masculinity. "That's where the thug in me came from," he boasted. At that point in his life, Afeni's entreaties, Mutulu's warnings went unheard. He was going from a one-day revolutionary to a one-man apocalypse. The incarcerated activist-intellectual Sanyika Shakur, who had corresponded with both Tupac and Mike Tyson during their prison terms, counseled Tupac about manly competition with other rappers. When it came to bad-ass bluffing, Sanyika advised "that the thing was getting too hostile. Either he had to smash on his foes or they'd smash him." But perhaps Sanyika's rhetoric had too many vengeful flourishes to convey the idea of careful, intellectual rebellion he intended. Tupac's boyish enthusiasm responded only to the cut throat ethic of the cynical Black street male. Its enlightened counterpart is the political prisoner's resentment, not his idealism.

Looking back, it appears that Tupac's outlook coarsened rather than clarified. His "Black youth's promise "got broken. The anger in *2pacalypse Now* is intended to represent that. It's Tupac's outspoken response to the mess of modern living. *2pacalypse Now*—well named after the artist's own, audacious sense of social responsibility—accurately reflects how kids feel, their simplified sense of political action.

By 1993, much of this was already encoded in vinyl and Tupac's listening lessons are apparent from the first track, "Young Black Male," which samples Ice Cube's 1990 "The Product." There are references to Public Enemy whose popularity had already peaked, but whose message was still real for Tupac; he built his debut on the political trail PE blazed. So there's delight in hearing hiphop cohere around itself, as though young Blacks were uniting intellectually. But a drawback becomes evident—for all PE's exciting rhetoric and vivid moral dilemmas, they deliver lectures, not education. KRS-One pompously refers to himself as "the teacher" but, in hiphop, that's the folly of the vain leading the blind. What's wanting is "America's Nightmare," a song that confuses PE and KRS-One with actual political activists. The hiphop generation wants to believe that its defiance has a social value even as it makes them rich. Listening to L.L. Cool J. thrive off "I'm Bad" made Tupac one of those hungry children he had not yet developed the moral sensibility to resist.

When Tupac begins "Young Black Male," repeating the chorus *"Hard like an erection,"* he's basing social identity on the most basic pride in self. Still at an early stage of self-awareness—the mirror stage—this infant of the revolution can only talk back to himself, and the tough talk has no reflection beyond facile encouragement. Fans thought Tupac spoke a great truth, but even that response is just the self-congratulation that is built into the record industry's youth marketing. If ghetto kids weren't so desperate for self-esteem, hiphop would never have succeeded as a quasi-political movement. Revolt replaced dancing as a hiphop subject because American society had become so untenable for Black youth that their urge to socialize was, in every sense, thwarted. Neil Young's ode to an aborted fetus, *"Here's one more kid that'll never go to school/Never get to fall in love/Never get to feel cool"* assumes

> I want when they see me they know everyday, when I'm breathin' . . .

teenage rights that society has denied to some—rights that many Black youths have had to snatch discourteously.

But this means living is half-living, half-conscious. *2pacalypse Now* only inflates Tupac's adolescent ire. There are only a few instances of teenage wit that provide the necessary scale to put kiddie-revolution in perspective. Instead, Tupac's invective borrows so liberally from the family heritage of activism that young listeners would be impelled to think a line like *"I don't give a fuck"* expresses soulful righteousness when it's merely brash. But Tupac's brashness can be engaging. He shared his youthful insolence with MTV:

I don't want to be 50 years old at a BET We Shall Overcome Achievement Awards. Uh uh, not me. I want when they see me they know everyday, when I'm breathin', it's for us to go farther. Every time I speak, I want the truth to come out. Every time I speak I want [them to] shiver, I don't want them to be like they know what I'm gonna say cuz it's [always] polite. They *know* what I'm gonna say? And even if I get in trouble, ain't that what we supposed to do? I'm

not sayin' I'm gonna rule the world, or I'm gonna change the world, but I guarantee that I will spark the brain that will change the world and that's our job.

The white folks at MTV may have swallowed this, been scared by it, taken in by what is really a complicated entertainer/politician shtick. Tupac went on about his job as hitmaker/provocateur:

It's to spark somebody else [who is] watchin' us. We might not be the ones, but lets not be selfish and because we not go' change the world let's not talk about how we should change it. I don't know how to change it but I know if I keep talkin about how dirty it is out here, somebody's gonna clean it up.

With all this bluster, Tupac gambles with *2pacalypse Now*'s charm; hiphop youth can claim the right to voice objection but only a few have earned the right, and even less have found the proper language. (Sister Souljah's underappreciated album 360 *Degrees of Power* displayed comprehensive political thinking, but she lacked Tupac's star appeal and didn't sell sex as an ideological weapon.)

"Wordz of Wisdom" uses protest as a way of feeling cool. The schoolboy of Sam Cooke's "Wonderful World" turns fashionably bitter. "Trapped's" tale of police brutality urges *"Naw, they can't keep the black man down."* When Tupac says *"I couldn't find a trace of equality/ Work me like a slave,"* he hits that pit of resentment every boy with holes in his pockets feels on the verge of adulthood. But when the narrative throws a boyhood fracas into the mix, politics are confused with incivility. Spite isn't a sufficient motivation for social change, yet change isn't Tupac's aim. *2pacalypse Now* is content with wrecking shit. The remorse that the Geto Boys articulated from "Mind Playin' Tricks On Me" on, never occurs to Tupac.

He thinks in pop terms, though. Eight producers, including Tupac himself, keep the tracks simple, from metronome beats to appropriating the melody of Stevie Wonder's "Part Time Love" for "Part Time Mutha." The bass voice he assumes for "Soulja's Story" is a projection of rebel attitude—a fantasy. And supposedly hard lines like "Mama told me there be days like this but I'm pissed/ 'Cuz it stays like this" are, in fact, platitudes of a new kind. Rapping dead-end scenarios to kids looking for a way out, Tupac offers fatalism as a reflex. Sister Souljah doesn't resort to that; neither does Chuck D; Ice Cube has learned better; Willie D, Scarface, and Bushwick Bill know even more, but none of them have Tupac's knack for the easy one-note concerto. He's smooth, cute, where Sister Souljah is hectoring. That's how he gets by with the theory—on "Wordz of Wisdom"—that 'Nigga' is not the nigga we're prone to fear but an acronym that means 'Not Ignorant Getting Goals Accomplished.'"

For a genuine politician this would be called devious, but in pop, it's just fatuous. Tupac means to reverse Black youth's value system—accepting the negative as a positive—but the goal he implies is brusque. No doubt Tupac was mightily impressed by the point of view expressed on N.W.A.'s 1989 album, *Straight Out of Compton*—an influential statement of the modern young Black male's temper. "A lot of what I been thinkin' about came alive when I heard 'Gangsta, Gangsta' and '—-tha Police,'" Tupac told a Bay Area homie. *2pacalypse Now's* "I Don't Give a Fuck" was easily accomplished after N.W.A.'s breakthrough. Tupac added fine-tuned variations on that Los Angeles group's severity. The title figured in Tupac's key dialogue in the movie *Juice;* he instinctively added it to the screenplay. But his dramatic sense is fully apparent on this track. It opens with a phone call, setting the scene of *"just another day in the life, G"* replete with homey communication and anger:

WHO'S THAT BEHIND THE TRIGGER?
WHO DO YOU FIGURE?
A MOTHERFUCKIN' NINE-INCH NIGGA
READY TO FUCK AND RIP SHIT UP
I'VE HAD ENOUGH
AND I JUST DON'T GIVE A FUCK

It still doesn't answer the problems Black youth face when trying to make their way through the world but, in the song's finale, Tupac pauses in his DJ Quik-style syncopation and declares "I gotta get my fuck-offs." He flips the finger to *the San Francisco police department, the Marin City Sheriff's department, the F.B.I., C.I.A., B.U.S.H., Amerika-ka-ka-ka, to all you red-neck prejudiced motherfuckas. Gay, insensitive, little-dicked bastards. Y'all can all kiss my ass and suck my dick and my Uncle Thomas' balls.*

"Fuck-offs" had become a virtual genre of hiphop; a specific variation on the rebellion first heard in British punk rock, they became an accepted part of music industry practice. But when Tupac ends "I Don't Give a Fuck" with a veritable echo—"punks, punks, punks, punks, punks, punks, punks"—he's using the partcular Black American meaning of the word. It's implicit sexism implies a value system that judges manliness as brute strength. His strategy brings social discomfort closer to personal affront than British punk ever dared, further antagonizing even his sympathizers. Rock critics may not know, but the homeboys understand.

A big irony catches this new level of impudence. On "Wordz of Wisdom" Tupac grumbles: *No Malcolm X in my history text/ Why's that?/ Because he tried to educate and liberate all Blacks/ Why is Martin Luther King in my book each week/ Cuz he taught all Blacks to get slapped/ And turn the other cheek.* For a revolutionary's son to voice such a simplification suggests he was given a slanted political education.

No teenager whose ego is boosted by Tupac's peevish tantrum knows enough to see its limits. Its cheekiness is too winning, a placebo. As the track fades over a lite-jazz background, Tupac epitomizes the development of this new, pissed-off satisfaction by wishing for "America's Nightmare" to come true. He casts it with assorted rap artists—Above the Law, Paris, Ice-T, Public Enemy—then links them to Mutulu Shakur, Assata Shakur, and Geronimo Pratt. His priorities are scattered; his earnestness is all wound up with family favoritism. The song stands as an artifact, a declaration of pop confusion.

REBEL FOR THE HELL OF IT

Talking about the new sense of comradery hiphop gave him, Tupac would tell MTV:

> We are businessmen, we're not animals. Its not like we're gonna see them and rush them. And jump on them if they see us and they want drama, we're gonna definitely bring it like only Death Row [Records] can bring it . . . [Next year] it's gonna be static for sure. What the rap audience ain't ready for is a real person. You know what I want to say: a real n-i-g-g-a. I'm comin' out 100 percent real. I ain't compromising anything. Anybody talk about me got problems you know what I m sayin'? It's gonna be straight up like I'm a street person. That's how I'm comin' at the whole world and I'm bein' real about it and I'm gonna grow with my music.

At an earlier MTV session, Tupac had worn a red hood pulled over his head to put his statements into an appropriately thuggish context:

```
The music that I make now? My next album?
Gonna be better and more slammin', you know
what I'm sayin'? But by the same token it's
gonna be more potent next year. And I don't
want no garbage coming my way ! Anybody talk
about me, anybody dis Digital Underground, they
got problems. Cuz we large and we all over the
country. Anybody dis us they gonna get stomped.
```

He's really acting now and the MTV interviewer soaks it all up—a cathode ray sponge. Riding the hype, Tupac televised a new revolution specifically for MTV and whoever else would listen. "That's word is bond," he assured his audience—and maybe his ancestors, too. "Cuz this is money. Cuz anybody try to take away Digital Underground's money as a whole, they got problems. We gonna suffocate 'em." Hearing this, other teens might salute, but Tupac's radical forefathers, sitting helpless in jail, worried.

On "Crooked Ass Nigga," Tupac flips out, snapping the chorus: *"Suddenly I see/ Some niggas that I don't like."* It's the origins of a vicious anti-brotherhood that fans like to excuse as just "complicated." It's easy to pump to a track like this without thinking; the intense rhythms of hiphop insure most rap records will have a groove. So Tupac is always automatically commercial, but the rhythms here don't keep your head ringing unless listeners invest them with a large amount of subjectivity, grooving to the notion of revenge and retaliation. That kind of audience identification is what's behind the frequent praise for *2Pacalypse Now's* best known track, "Brenda's Got a Baby"—it pleases the hiphop heads who cold-shouldered De La Soul's brilliantly dramatic character studies ("Millie Pulled a Pistol on Santa," "My Brother's a Basehead") on *De La Soul Is Dead.*

Tupac begins the song's story, *"Brenda's got a baby but barely got a brain,"* then proceeds to tell *"how it affects our whole community."* Eventually this tale of a seduced and abandoned teenage girl blames her for being dumb and giving the ghetto a bad rap. After giving birth, *"She didn't know what to throw away or what to keep."* The only tender verse says: *"She didn't realize how the baby had her eyes."* Pop fans reminded of The Sex Pistols' "Bodies" will note Tupac replaces political scorn with a simple pathetic portrait of moral impropriety. "Brenda" is actually less forgiving than "Crooked Ass Nigga." Young Tupac's boyishness shows in the moral weight he holds against wayward girls rather than bad boys.

"Part Time Mutha" also makes a mixed indictment: *"Cindy was my dope fiend mother"* (perhaps an early peek at Tupac's Oedipal anger). By using the terms and limits of teenage understanding—rapping intuitively as the child of a teen-age mother—Tupac goes right to the heart of his audience's sympathies. So that even his description of Brenda's stupidity—*"Didn't have a job/ Tried to sell crack/ End up gettin' robbed"*—gets the intended emotional effect. To hear this as sympathetic is to look at Tupac's hardness with naivete. The moaning female chorus sounds sentimental, which accounts for the record rise to Number Three on the rap charts, but it's as deceptive as the trite melodrama in a Hughes Brothers' movie—and *they* shot the music video for "Brenda Got a Baby."

By this time, Tupac had developed Bay Area friends and music industry associates like the Hughes Brothers who, in their own version of neo-Horatio Alger Black culture, encouraged Tupac in any behavior and attitude that would get him paid. With Albert and Allen Hughes, Tupac approached the hiphop depiction of contemporary Black life as marketable depression. In contrast to the Hughes Brothers' comfortable upbringing on Detroit's middle-class westside and in Pomona, California, Tupac's street background and extreme behavior found another eager audience. Excited by his willingness to impress, the Hughes Brothers crafted, in the Brenda video and others they filmed with Tupac, an aesthetic dependent on debased Black circumstances and behavior. This early form of exploitation would not be the basis for a long lasting friendship; Tupac and the Hughes Brothers were destined to become courtroom adversaries. (Producer Michael G. Moye told the special Jim Crow issue of *Movieline* Magazine that the movie that changed his life was the Hughes Brothers' *Dead Presidents*: "We have seen the enemy and it is us.") Tupac's early video efforts were built on the shaky ground of stereotype and jive. While L.L. Cool J., DJ Quik, and Public Enemy give *2pacalypse Now* its warmest, wittiest flavor, these other pop inspirations are the first hint that Tupac's youth appeal might also be his undoing.

A Bay Area hiphop journalist described uneasy moments in the first flush of Tupac's success:

> **I remember Tupac best as an elated young man with his first real apartment, a one-bedroom joint in Oakland. It was 1991, and Tupac had just returned from a world-wide (hotel after hotel) tour. Before that, he'd often slept on recording-studio couches and on the floors of various apartments rented by members of Digital Underground.**

A party was in order to celebrate the little bit of money Tupac had made from working, touring, recording, and video shoots.

> **Tupac showed us all around, pointing out this knickknack and that, telling us for how much and from where he purchased his sheets and towels, telling us without telling us of his profound relief at having a place of his own."**

He also had two guns prominently displayed on the lower tier of the glass-top coffee table. As the party went on, with drinks passed around:

> **Tupac picked up one of the guns and turned it around in his hands, inspecting its barrel and trigger, bragging excitedly about its ability to do damage.**

There's a familiarity in this remembrance that is common to all people watching another's rise in the social order. It also recalls that scene in Scorsese's *Who's That Knocking at My Door* where a gun suggests a lethal potential. Tupac was showing off to a group of friends:

> **who had all fed him . . . picked him up from desolate bus stops in the middle of the night, listened to his poems before they were raps, and introduced him to girls.**

But this same group, impressed by Tupac's first steps up the showbiz and social ladder, were setting the stage for the way Tupac would perform for the rest of his life.

> **No one said anything. It was a combination of tact and trepidation that made us pretend to sip the gritty liquid and watch as Tupac, gun in hand began to bounce off the walls of his new kingdom.**

Tupac found glory to be fickle. *2pacalypse Now* had sold over 500,000 copies—qualifying for a Gold Album from the Recording Industry of America—but shortly after its release, the past made a claim on Tupac. In Oakland where, almost fifteen years earlier, the Panthers had organized in response to police brutality, Tupac was arrested for jaywalking. He filed a $10 million lawsuit against the Oakland police for alleged brutality. He said of the incident "I know about this from what my stepfather told me. They fuck with me just on principle." He fit the image of the Young Black Male he rapped about in *2pacalypse Now*. The future—Hollywood—was claiming him, too.

CHAPTER 6
a star is bought

hollywood was looking

for street Blacks. *Juice*, the latest attempt to bring hiphop culture to the big screen, was based on a script by New York playwright Gerard Brown to be directed by Ernest Dickerson, the cinematographer on Spike Lee's *Do the Right Thing* and *Mo' Better Blues*. After the box office success of *New Jack City* in 1989, *Juice* went into production to catch the latest pop wave.

A casting call went out early in 1990 to hire actors who could fit Brown and Dickerson's vision of Harlem Black youth; word of the casting went from coast to coast. Money B first tried out for the role of Bishop in *Juice*. As Digital Underground's second rapper, it was more than likely he might fit the producers image of rap authenticity; the role of Bishop was conceived as the era's quintessential bad boy. Tupac came along on the audition just for the ride, not to

Adger W. Cowans/Everett Collection

interfere with Money B's plans, but counting on the producers wanting some genuine street Black in a small part or to authenticate the movie's background. Instead, Tupac got the role and his portrayal of Bishop became the movie's core.

This was to be Tupac's first real chance to act since Baltimore. Now, with actual music industry credentials to support his efforts, Tupac's creative interests were coming together. As Bishop, Tupac would be able to vent the restless aggression that was keeping him alive, whether he was hustling dope for survival or angling for recognition in rap. These activities were themselves forms of acting. "It's what I gotta do, and I'mo do it good enough to keep my Black ass off welfare," a Bay area acquaintance remembers Tupac saying. His determination shocked many more-laid-back or pragmatic West Coast colleagues, but Mac Dre, one of the Underground rap artists, understood Tupac's zeal. "For him to be recognized as a player by someone on top of the game gave him encouragement." And Tupac responded with an alacrity that almost suggested an artificially assisted enthusiasm. In *Juice*, that macho drive would prove to be the speed that thrills.

Yes, Tupac's debut, *Juice*, glamorizes and encourages violence. By turning complex contemporary African American life into the kind of movie clichés people are used to seeing (and, therefore, don't give much thought to), *Juice* makes the traps and temptations of ghetto life seem attractive. The eagerness of white commentators to defend the film against claims that it inspires violence in youthful audiences, shows their distance from African American reality. Their ignorance about the causes of Black-on-Black violence is just what *Juice* corroborates. The protagonists in *Juice* flatter b-boy swagger by linking it up with the familiar hijinks of action movies. *Juice's* supposed moral lesson is indistinguishable from its fascination with the easily exploitable aspects of Black urban life. *Juice* revels but offers no revelation.

Only one moment really works: It's the casual encounter with a crime-in-progress that begins as a friendly reunion between neighborhood fellas. "You want a piece of this?" the perp asks in a tone that clearly defines the comradery that exists even within lawless, hostile social situations. That's a pretty original and, these days, highly plausible scenario. Screenwriter Gerard Brown and director Ernest Dickerson wisely let the moment's absurdity happen without undue emphasis. Their nineties variation on *Mean Streets* must be understood as *Crazy Streets*—an update of Martin Scorsese as well as Piri Thomas.

Juice combines urban subculture and social horror genres through authentic details common to hiphop. The story of four Harlem young men ensnared in violence has a harder edge than Joseph B. Vasquez' *Hangin' With the Homeboys*, yet both dramatize the humanity that gets lost in white media statistics about urban youth. Still, it's just as cliché-ridden. Brown, Dickerson, and Vasquez face the problem of making personal experience and observation fit the format of commercial cinema. And here's the problem: How does the cultural revolution of hiphop get transferred to feature films without condescending to

Tupac Shakur
in Juice.

the audience? *Juice* would have been a really good film if, somehow, it could have taken a cue from Hank Shocklee's score (especially the amazing title track performed by Eric B and Rakim) which was truly innovative. From *Boyz N the Hood* and *Straight Out of Brooklyn* to *Juice*, none of these films shows the invention, passion, intelligence—the art—of the music that serves as their background and/or inspiration.

It's plain that the filmmakers are trying to attract moviegoers who may not be familiar with the narrative innovations of rap, but doing so falsifies the experience that they're trying to convey. Rap's innovation comes out of language and narrative that had to be reshaped and reconceived to contain the language and ideas of the life it derives from. These movies are carrying that life back to the domain from which rap artists rescued it. Where *Boyz N the Hood* and *Juice* succeed as conventional movie narratives—in moments of mawkish misery that show young men suffering—they simultaneously fail as original works of art. The implicit politics of making African American ironies into all-American truths are watered down by story lines that don't resonate.

White critics may applaud these films because the tales have been sapped of the energy and nuance—the juice—that is essential to their troubled difference from the white world. But when Black audiences lap up these paltry features, they submit to the very problem the films are about: Conventional plots and conventional moralism restrict artists who must describe a new set of experiences and, apparently, an altered moral code.

Juice divides interest among a crew—Q (Omar Epps), an aspiring rap disc jockey; Rahaeem (Khalil Kain), an unwed father with slick delusions; Steel (Jermaine Hopkins), the babyish, overweight kid; and Bishop (Tupac), the gangster. You already know which of these characters is going to be the most interesting—and you know that the conventional way moviemakers handle the bad guy will give no real insight into his character but keep the focus on the "excitement" of his acts. Maybe Gerard Brown backed away from identifying and exploring Bishop for fear of making a hero out of him, but the concentration on good boy Q misrepresents the film's real interests. *Juice* means to exploit the notion of corrupt, violent power by showing the weakness felt by young men who don't have it but who desperately want to control their lives.

By reducing the story's tension to a showdown between careerist Q and impulse-killer Bishop, Brown oversimplifies the choices that the ghetto offers. His theatrical simplification reduces real moral dilemma to the same old chase scenes, fistfights, and gun battles without any moral or political underpinning. There's not enough subtext in *Juice*, none of the religious or cultural background that made *Mean Streets* specific (and transcendent). By diffusing interest and not looking too closely at any of these characters, Brown and Dickerson may have intended to encompass more of the Black urban experience. That emphasis may contain a healthy sense of community but it doesn't excuse the well-acted but insufficient views of family life and police brutality. But it may, in fact, be this avoidance of focus on the specific that accounts for the abundant clichés.

When the boys decide to rob a store with no personal motivation (or dramatic preparation), *Juice* seems to be fulfilling TV- news stereotypes. Brown and Dickerson aren't doing the work of showing what the robbery *means*. Even a tense, beautifully hectic fight scene in Steel's living room goes dumb. Bishop jumps up with a startling ferocity that is supposed to be unfathomable, yet this kind of lethal behavior has not been credibly linked to the group's general passivity.

Reality and genre are unevenly mixed here. Still, Brown and Dickerson come the closest anyone ever has to examining the puzzle of Black malice. It comes through *Juice*'s hyperbole, but it shouldn't be mystified like the Robert Johnson legends that white critics love. We need hard-minded street sense about this type of guy, but Bishop just gets nightmarish. And Tupac's star power actually deflects insight in the speech that launched so many nineties Black Hollywood stereotypes:

I don't give a fuck! I don't give a fuck about you. I don't give a fuck about Steel. I don't give a fuck about Rahaeem, either. I don't give a fuck about myself! Look, I ain't shit and I ain't never gonna be shit and you less of a man than me.

Tupac's force carries this scene and several others; he's a potent actor who clearly knows the secrets of macho fronting. He chomps at the bit when watching *White Heat* on TV ("That motherfucker took his destiny in his own hands!") But talent and force isn't a justification for ignoring how Bishop's anger just pops out of nowhere. Bishop's behavior is cut off from reason, suggesting a desperate freedom to young viewers. (And scaring the establishment; Paramount Pictures airbrushed the gun Bishop holds from the movie's promotion campaign.)

If any movie has plied the male teen mystery carefully, it must be *Rebel without a Cause* in which Jim's (James Dean's) sense of freedom was an aspect of his higher sensitivity, his superior expression of love. Tupac makes Bishop spectacular, but the movie doesn't crack him open. Juice replaces psychological depth with the oldest action-movie bits: a dead man's grasping hand; the jolting appearance of an enemy; and the proverbial bad aim at close range (this time, at least, in an elevator!) It may not take much to bilk $7.50 from the homeboy audience, but it takes some dedication and imagination to do more justice to their lives than Brown and Dickerson (among many others) are providing.

"*Juice* is about four kids and their coming of age," Tupac told a reporter "It's not a hiphop movie. It's a real good movie that happens to have hiphop in it." He was well aware of the pigeon-holing that goes on, even within the hiphop industry itself. Once again Tupac saw acting as a way out, a means of transcending the limits others placed on him.

"If *Juice* was made in the sixties, it would've depicted whatever was down in the sixties. My character is Roland Bishop, a psychotic, insecure, very violent, very short-tempered individual." Tupac's assessment is invaluable; its short circuits all the sentimentality that commentators have attached to Bishop, recognizing that Bishop is a means to articulate the rage of young Black men. Apparently, he was quite capable of approaching the stereotype and aware of just how far to take it, aware of what it meant, and the possible effect it would have. *Juice* gave Tupac another opportunity to get the news out about how he and other stressed-out Black American males felt.

Hiphop fans bought Tupac's image in *Juice* because they recognized it. Identification with Bishop was part sentiment; then, self-affirmation; and then, like rap itself, justification. The soundtrack was replete with the moment's best, hardest hiphop—an exhilarating title track by Eric B and Rakim, a score produced by Public Enemy's Hank Shocklee, even a track from the avant-rap band, Son of Bazerk.

When it came time to hype the movie, the Bay Area was ready to honor its native hiphop son. Alex Mejia, a remixer/producer for radio station KMEL recalls :

> **We put a little event together with 'Pac and Digital Underground and we definitely let people know that this was going to be the movie to beat for the summer. He came through and that's when I was really able to see his star quality. He was like a magnet. Everyone was just astonished that he was there. Mad autographs. . .**

Leila Steinberg also knew the moment had arrived. "Everyone has their thing that gives them their recognition. I'm talking about that beyond-star quality." Shock G and Money B of Digital Underground also gave it up. "Watch out for this dude. He's sewing up some stuff he's about to do and he's about to explode."

CHAPTER 7 contrasts

apart from the entertainment pages, it was trouble that first put Tupac's face in the news. Glamour would make it seem to belong there. On August 22, 1992, at a fiftieth anniversary benefit celebration in Marin City, Tupac had a confrontation—a grudge match that resulted in a six-year-old boy getting shot in the head. The weapon used was traced to Tupac's half-brother, Maurice (Mopreme) Harding, who was arrested, then released; but the injured boy's family filed a civil suit. This was the worst of several catastrophes and brought Tupac his first notoriety.

In Texas that spring, 19-year-old Ronald Ray Howard shot a Texas Trooper, claiming *2pacalypse Now*, which was in his car's tapedeck at the time, had inspired him. Months later, Vice President Dan Quayle denounced Tupac, urging Interscope Records to pull *2pacalypse Now* from record stores. His soundbite: "This music has no place in our society."

Hiphop celebrity was turning Tupac into Public Enemy Number One—with a bullet: In March, 1993, a Hollywood limousine driver accuses Tupac of using drugs in the vehicle. A fight follows; Tupac is arrested but charges are dropped. Less than a month later, in Lansing, Michigan, Tupac is arrested and sentenced to ten days in jail for an altercation in which he swung a baseball bat at a local rapper.

Tupac's profile was almost as visible in newsprint as in music videos. Hiphop was establishing its own dubious standards for stardom and authenticy based on the ruffneck image favored in lyrics. Tupac brought reality and show-biz together when he stormed a Hughes Brothers' video shoot with his "posse," threatening the twin directors. Reports attributed the dispute to the Hughes Brothers first engaging then dismissing Tupac as the lead of the hiphop movie that would be their theatrical debut, *Menace II Society*. Both sides felt the other had gained from their previous collaborations, but neither respected that fact or felt obligated by it. *Menace II Society* finally opened in the summer of 1993. The Hughes Brothers themselves became hiphop minutemen, stars of the moment, but by then Tupac had outstripped them and every actor in that movie. Trouble had not only made Tupac's name; it had made his face recognizable everywhere.

Tupac's second solo album, *Strictly For My N.I.G.G.A.Z.* had the effect of imprinting Tupac's image in the daily fantasies of early-nineties hiphoppers. This trained actor and former member of the randy Digital Underground was still a minor figure until *Keep Your Head Up*, the video from *Strictly for My N.I.G.G.A.Z.*, became a hit. (The live-wire fascination of seeing Tupac on screen rapping is best matched on the album when Tupac teams up with Ice Cube, Ice-T and Live Squad for cameo raps.) "Keep Your Head Up"'s rapt appeal to women turned a hiphop roustabout into a Hollywood-style sheikh— a romantic image that would eventually overwhelm even the public alarm at Tupac's real-life criminal charges for sexual battery. Tupac became a star by advocating romance with respect: telling women to keep their pride, men to mind their bedside manners.

"Keep Your Head Up" is one of hiphop's signal performances. It combines masculine love with social propriety. This is rare in a form as renegade and disorderly as rap. Tupac's hardness makes the tenderness so easy to take, it *seems* unsentimental. Starting with the abused "darker" sisters as well as the *"sisters on welfare/when don't nobody else care,"* with a plea in his voice he makes a case for the world to respect Black women, while also pledging his troth to those women who may be listening. With troubadour shrewdness, Tupac returns verbal seduction to the provenance of what—when Afeni and Billy Garland and Mutulu were kids—was originally meant by the term "rapping." Several generations of disrespected women swooned to "Keep Your Head Up"'s entreaty:

I wonder why we take from

our women

while we rape our women

Do we hate our women

I think it's time we kill

for our women

Time we heal our women

Be real to our women

Neither Public Enemy's magnificent ode to Black women, "Revolutionary Generation," nor Salt'N Pepa's and En Vogue's "Whatta Man" had quite the common touch that "Keep Your Head Up" manages. From Tupac's inspired use of the "Oooh Child" melody to his steady, courtly appeal, it was the perfect record to redress rap's all-too-frequent misogyny. Pop makes these preachments sound like promises; a star like Tupac can make audiences believe it sheerly by a charming, seductive presence.

And here's the problem: Throughout *Strictly for My N.I.G.G.A.Z.*, Tupac, on a hellraising jag, presents contradictory attitudes, that rebut the communal, feel-good emotions of "Keep Your Head Up." On "Tupac's Theme," he repeats a motto, "I was born in this society. There's no way you can expect me to be a perfect person. I'm gonna do what I'm gonna do." It sounds earnest but it only reminds us how young he is, how much more of the world there is for him to experience, learn about, and put on the record. Tupac's reckless credo is sincerely at odds with his "righteousness."

Strictly For My N.I.G.G.A.Z. compliments Tupac's real-life troubles, seeking an artistic response to them. "I can't set the record straight in the studio," Tupac told a reporter. That adjustment is clear on "I Get Around," a reunion with Digital Underground that describes Tupac's insouciant player attitude. Sampling Zapp's "Computer Land," it glorifies the pleasures of hiphop highlife. A boy's thing, the fun includes money, women, and the sharing of both—a hiphop fancy based in the wild life of touring, looking away from its hardships to the ease that one fantasizes celebrity to be. When Tupac chants in between Shock G and Money B, "loose lips sink ships," his fellatio metaphor also urges his boys to keep the secret of their fantasy-sweet life. The "round and round we go" chorus at first sounds orgiastic but, with repetition, hints at exhaustion to come.

But back-to-back with "I Get Around," "Papa'z Song" rebukes the playboy dream with unexpected venom. There's no movement of mind that connects these tunes—it's sheer juxtaposition, sheer contradiction. Tupac put all his fears of abandonment, his resentment towards the revolving-door role models and fairweather fakes who churned up his childhood into this song. "Couldn't stand UP!/To his own responsibility"—the startled emphasis on "up" suggests Tupac's discontent with masculine failure, his father's moral impotence:

Had to play catch by myself
Once outside a pitiful plight so I pray for a starry night

> Please send me a pops before puberty
> The things I wouldn't do to see a piece of family unity

A harried tune, it does as much for ghetto bastards as "Keep Your Head Up" does for underappreciated women.

It's undeniable that this song divulges troubling autobiography. The rhyme scheme is slack, the vitriol spewed out rather than constructed. Yet Tupac is able to encompass an entire generation's woe—a star's gift. In a twist that recalls the bitter vocal shift in the second half of Stevie Wonder's "Living For the City," Tupac alters his voice, gives it a horrific testosterone depth, to portray the excuses made by the absentee parent. The guitar picking underneath is poignantly gentle, perhaps too yielding to give the shock that is needed to condemn this all-too-common male treachery. Instead it's the sound of breakdown and almost-forgiveness. That bellowing father's voice bears an uncomfortable resemblance to the one on *2pacalaypse Now's* "Soulja's Story," where the bass notes don't echo distance but vibrate with iron-willed determination. Between these two tracks, Tupac exposes his ambivalence, keeping the listener unaware of his split—perhaps an effort to keep the truth from himself. "Papa'z Song" is raw, unprocessed pain not yet fully understood, a freshly opened wound.

After the shootings and arrests that preceded *Strictly For My N.I.G.G.A.Z.,* Tupac tried to deal with the troubles exploding around him and inside him. Raised to believe in absolutes, he has difficulty comprehending his own ambivalence. Tupac had figured out, "I know nobody does right all the time but, when it comes to the kids and crew, you gotta be there for 'em." It was a theory based on his own experience, plus his idea of how the imperfect world ought to work. He sought a solution in art: in movies, in videos and, most of all, in rap. Tupac told a reporter:

I have a group and a program called the Underground Railroad. I want to strengthen it. The concept behind this is the same concept behind Harriet

> Tubman, to get my brothers who might be into drug dealing or whatever it is
> that's illegal or who are disenfranchised by today's society—I want to get them
> back by turning them onto music. It could be R&B, hiphop, or pop, as long as
> I can get them involved. While I'm doing that, I'm teaching them to find a love
> for themselves so they can love others and do the same thing we did for them
> to others.

This program eventually turned into Thug Life, the short-lived rap group that Tupac sponsored. In 1992, as a sign of commitment, Tupac had the acronym he had developed with Mutulu tattooed across his abdomen. As the Underground Railroad program evolved into the Thug Life movement, Tupac took in followers across the country, many from the East Coast, including Treach from Naughty by Nature, The Notorious B.I.G., and Randy "Sretch" Walker," his brother Mopreme, The Rated R, Macadoshis, and Big Syke!, a rapper from Englewood, New Jersey. Big Syke! recalls:

> He was no different from anybody else. Me and Tupac hit it off. I was like 'Oh,
> man, he's a little nut! This nigga's a little nut! And that's what I loved about him.
> He ain't gon' back down, he might overtalk sometimes, but little homies do
> that. It was the same shit that all of us do. But he was in front of the world
> doing it. That's the only thing separating him from any other Black young God
> running around in these neighborhoods. He had the opportunity.

Big Syke! claims to have wised Tupac up about street life, while Tupac hooked him up careerwise."See, if you listen to 'Pac's music before he got to Thug Life, it was more of a Panther-type thought. When he got to Thug Life, it was like, this is where the street, the thugs, the gangstas, the crack, all this [was]." Big Syke! says the group's album *Thug Life Vol 1* was tamed by the record company. "They had watered it down so much, it wasn't even half of what it was when it first started." Still, it carried Tupac's creativity along. Even

Big Syke! was impressed: "He loved doing music, man! He would just do it like that. He'll write a song in like fifteen, twenty minutes." Tupac wrote and recorded with an urgent need to express himself. He encouraged Big Syke! to release himself through rap, as he did. "After my homeboy Big Cato that was like my brother got killed, we went straight to the studio, he was like 'Nigga take your pain out on this song.' That's what we did and it came out the bomb."

CHAPTER 8
viewing the body

"shockingly handsome," is how *Newsweek* magazine described Shakur when he and Snoop Doggy Dogg had concurrent run-ins with the courts in the fall of 1993. "Tupac, with his unforgettable, big brown eyes and his radiant, natural charm . . . " a male MTV reporter fawned, while reporting how the star waited to be sentenced for threatening video director Alan Hughes.

Tupac had dealt with the pressure of such attention ever since high school. A Baltimore classmate remembers Tupac looking at first abashed at a couple of girls who thrilled to his New York exoticism; then, going all out for the admiration. This awareness easily recalls the way a shy teen might react to a group of girls telling him he's "fine"—he may dress better, brush his teeth more often and, if at all "lucky," he may win the sexual experience—and confidence—to change the very way he walks. He'll appreciate his body's commodity, take care of his "instrument."

Such awareness operates deep within the image of teen idols and is intuited in the charm of movie icons who have finessed many levels of public adoration. Yet movies have barely begun to romanticize the Black version of this experience. Hollywood has shied away from promoting Black romantic actors—it would go against the white supremacy Hollywood has created to endorse. "They ain't never seen a nigga like me!" Tupac boasted, as he advanced on Tinseltown.

While Tupac's rapping endeared him to the core hiphop audience, others, less knowing, admired his rap style. Critic R.J. Smith observed, "His rapping technique was leaden and hadn't grown much over four records." What that assessment leaves out is a fact rap fans knew instinctively—Tupac was, above all else, a star, a performer who is good to look at and embodies instantly recognizable emotions.

That's why Tupac's performances on the big screen—in *Juice, Poetic Justice, Above the Rim, Gridlock'd,* and several of his own music videos—are so refreshing. Startling, but not shocking. He commands attention for his wide, dark-rimmed eyes (hooded, yet alert), his wiry sway—-and. his ability to hit a precise emotion. Tupac extended that wide, tumescent prominence of his nose in the sensual aggression of his *I Get Around* video. The title understated Tupac's wildness while the video used satyriasis as a metaphor for uncontrollable mischief. A star's sexual prerogative and a hoodlum's social threat were combined in one rap icon: Tupac prancing around shirtless, the phrase "Thug Life" tattooed across his abdomen.

Tough behavior and soft moral sentiments may be part of youthful confusion, but often, the final effect is that the sentiments sound like hollow platitudes. That's why stars cannot be followed as role models; they're often just frontin'—as when Queen Latifah, to whom Tupac pays tribute on "Representin' '93," raps the hypocritical "U.N.I.T.Y." yet still produces ruffneck, female-bashing artists on her own label. At least Rick James meant what he sang in "Super

Above
the Rim

Freak." Much of this gets resolved with maturity. Latifah's featured role in the movie *Set It Off* comes close to a compensation: the film's insulting fantasy of Black female bank robbers is interesting only for Latifah's upfront portrayal of a butch lesbian—a role that made even hiphop cognoscenti drop their jaws along with their faith in gossip when confronted with Latifah's bold feminist principle.

Similarly, Tupac would complicate his Young Black Male image through the sensitivity of his characterization of Lucky, the struggling young postal worker and single father in *Poetic Justice*. Music video and movies give rappers a physical authority that audio recordings can't match. Tupac's body, put on display, was his area of absolute control.

upac's visual, physical presence had become a fact of hiphop culture by '93 on the basis of his impact in *Juice* and most of all, in his music video *I Get Around*. In *Poetic Justice*, Tupac's big screen appearance amounted to a confirmation of what the attentive pop audience already knew. "Nice nose!" Tyra Ferrell moaned in *Poetic Justice,* summing up Tupac's physical attributes in what will be remembered as his only lead film role. Ferrell's exclamation articulated Tupac's appeal—even when he lay one-hundred-and-fifty pounds, five-feet-eight inches on the coroner's slab—locating it largely in his sexual allure. Her enthusiasm stood out from all of the film's other dialogue because it also accounted for his magnetic pull on audiences. As she spoke it, public response to Tupac was in the air, his stardom—the irresistable rise of his renown—was imminent.

Movies, the deluxe part of the pop apparatus, put Tupac's body on the block. Cinema's exploitative terms seem never to change, whether glorifying the working class Irish gall of James Cagney, Dustin Hoffman's urban Jewish tenacity, or Al Pacino's dolorous Italian intensity—a star becomes an archetype and "an original," as one critic described the young Barbra Streisand. A certain amount of selling is inevitable in this showbiz contract; it can enhance or destroy a performer depending upon his/her ability to cope with lifestyle changes and control career opportunities. "I am my own commodity," Elizabeth Taylor testified before a congressional hearing in the eighties—a memorable statement that contrasts the axiom "My body is my instrument," said by actors seeking an analogy to endow their profession with the craft and esteem associated with musicianship.

By '93 most pop audiences were aware of the performer/object puzzle. The audience's full appreciation of Tupac's "qualities" includes an awareness of his possible commercial use—their enjoyment complies with his exploitation. Audiences depend on human display and take pleasure from it; but it may exact an unforeseeable price of the performer who is focused in the world's attention. The stud in Tupac's left nostril suggests he'd taken notice of his nose's sleek protuberance and its sensual affect long before Ferrell made mention of it. (That line was either improvized by the actress or customized by screenwriter-director John Singleton to fit Tupac's image.) Such evidence of style is always a sign of self-awareness. Afeni herself wore a nose ring, ratifying the ornament for Tupac as an emblem of pride, suitable adornment for an African American prince. The showiness of public performance—as when Tupac and other rappers readily mention the act of recording, touring, and being watched—becomes a subject of the songs themselves. Rappers pointedly emphasize their deliberate, showy artistry—they are bejeweled with creativity. Their bodies shine, their records vibrate. The spectacular sense of music as beats, riffs as samples, rhymes as familiar quotations, all demonstrate a new value accorded to art—and at the same time to human endeavor.

"*We were meant to be kept down/ Just can't understand why we get respect now*" Tupac rapped against the restraint and disparagement Black artists endure. But hiphop's boastful determination adds a layer of existential complexity to the task. A drummer can pound a beat simply but it carries a historical echo. Tupac knew this; it's apparent in the way he borrowed L.L. Cool J. and Public Enemy beats on his first album. In the same way the hiphop generations make their own music with subtle or blatant associations with its past, wearing cultural totems like crowns.

Until the proven, lucrative benefits of hiphop, there was no Hollywood image of Black youth anyone could readily put a name to. Earlier showbiz images came from the stage or the record industry—young Sammy Davis, Jr., Frankie Lymon, Michael Jackson. It remained for Tupac to embody on screen young Black male tensions and ambitions (following Ice Cube's *Boyz N the Hood* debut) and an assortment of young b-boy dreamboats, nice guys, and ruffnecks in music video.

Throwing himself on screen—twenty feet tall, fifty feet wide—as a quicksilver villain or heart-aching lover, he sparked a new audience's breathless response—particularly in women but also in men, startled by the masculine impact of Tupac's image. The sexual and social potential his body represented had to jolt even Tupac, himself, especially in that proverbial Junior High School way. It's the existential shock of being recognized by others for abilities—or fantasies—one may not have ever imagined.

Tupac's next step is either to fully accept his effect or carefully accommodate what he perceives as its demands. The archetype/original thus both follows a style and sets it. That's the story told by Tupac's body art. "It's my body," Tupac told a friend, when he got his nose stud. "And I'm gonna do with it what I want, not what somebody tells me I ought to do with it!"

Elaborately tattooed, he made his connection to the fast-growing nineties fad of self-inscription; though obviously, by the time Tupac's body took its final bullet, the selective decorations had become much more than simple accessories. Like the exotic stud in his nose, Tupac's tattoos signified his objections to pop conformity. Script and design spread across his flesh like routes on a road map.

Tattoos communicate to the cognoscenti—a rose means love, a dagger symbolizes danger—the inner life becomes emblematic. "I'm not gonna explain all these to you," Tupac snapped at a reporter. "Read 'em yourself. You can read, can't you!" His tattoos put his inside thoughts, outside—the secret me for you to see. Still, not really me—just me frustrated, straining to be something *more* than a skinny mama's boy looking for daddy. Tattoos built of ink and fantasy portrayed Tupac's psyche in certain arch, idealized, enigmatic figures. He traded his own skin for an exoskeleton.

On Tupac's brown, muscled flesh, one can read the same structure of bewildered desperation that each year peeks out more eerily from Michael Jackson's emaciated frame. This personal terror is also evident in Prince's recent cosmetic graffiti, "Slave"—a very hiphop notion (along with Prince's gun-shaped microphone), it abuses political history to make a mere corporate point. Prince invokes slavery to deflect from his privilege and to justify his petulance, same as many rappers do. Jackson, Prince, and Tupac are related in their internalized confusion about showbiz and racial politics. Sixties soul stars conformed their images—looked like interchangeable negroes.

With new opportunities to articulate their anger and effect some control

Raymond Boyd/Michael Ochs

ARMOND WHITE

over destiny, Black pop stars in the eighties and nineties—unlike their predecessors, Cooke, Redding, Tex, Pickett, Gaye—shunned conformity. Instead they choose *outré* identities in an attempt to hide psychic pain behind physical—often sexual—insignia, curiously reversing the old blackface compulsion. Hiphop's earlier, presumably innocent days, featured Melle Mel of Grandmaster Flash and the Furious Five taking to leather-and-chains, emblems of sadomasochism; Melle Mel flaunted his desire for strength to compensate feelings of weakness and oppression. Tupac similarly chose the S&M markings favored in prisons to signify his affinity with hard-luck brothers. This put "inside" stress on the outside—on his body and in the world.

Tupac's markings were doubly meaningful: they created a tribal code and by the unique methods of primitive tattooing—prisoners use a cassette motor and guitar string setup to put messages in flesh—they indicate music industry indenture. These elaborate ideograms are intended to make the bearer exclusive, hardcore, and sexy. But tattooing gave Tupac a costume like any other. His array included:

- **THUG LIFE** across abs
- 2pac on right pec
- 50 niggaz over sternum
- Nefertiti over left pec
- outlaw on right forearm
- Christ in flames and crown of thorns on right biceps
- Serpent with jaws open on right shoulder
- PLAYAZ on nape of neck
- Fuck The World across trapazoids
- German cross with Exodus 18:11 across back
- LAUGH NOW with mask of comedy
- cry later with mask of tragedy on lower sides of back
- *Fuck the World* in script across shoulder blades

This *Modern Primitives* icon that Tupac made of himself is likely to mean as much to his generation as the famous George Lois photograph of Muhammad Ali as St. Sebastian meant to another. In the nineties, slings and arrows are replaced by provocative words. (When New York's Whitney Museum mounted its scandalous *Black Male* show in 1995, it featured a photo of Tupac—gun in waistband, scowl on his face, flipping the bird with his right hand—that messed with his wider social stereotype by subtly implicating him in what is actually a gay porn pose.) Tupac's engraved body was as marked by superstitions, traditional beliefs, and delirium as Robert DeNiro's Matthew Cady in *Cape Fear*. Tupac's torso looked the way rap record samples sound—ideas overlapping, bumping into each other, cultural graffiti blotting out nature, contentment. The same wild, jumbled excess crowds the liner notes on his albums:

THANX 2 ALL THE TRUE MOTHERFUKAZ—THANX 4 BEING DOWN 4 MY COME UP NO NAMES NEEDED FUCK THE MEDIA! FUCK QUAYLE! THANK THE LORD! I FINALLY MADE IT OUT OF THE GHETTO, WHO'S NEXT! FUCK ALL POLICE, SKINHEADS, NAZI WHATEVER!!

As a man thinketh so is his body. Tattooed 'Pac was a visual collage, a paroxysm of codes, a walking emblem of contemporary chaos. To get this across Tupac endured having THUG LIFE written across his abdomen. He was in love with acronyms, from the one on his album cover (N.I.G.G.A.Z. meaning Never Ignorant Getting Goals Accomplished) to the one on his gut (T.H.U.G.L.I.F.E. meaning The Hate U Give Little Infants Fucks Everyone). Rap wasn't enough to convey these messages. Tupac believed in what he could see. Hollywood went along with the extremes of this self-illustrated man. He fashioned his own body to be read.

CHAPTER 9
poetic justice

**"THE WHOLE WORLD IS SWINGIN'
FROM JANET JACKSON'S BRA STRAP"**
—2pac

tupac wanted to be a movie star. That's one of the revelations his Bay Area manager Steinberg recalled to *4080 Magazine*. His ambitions only sharpened after the exposure and reception he got from *Juice* and his music videos. "He had this incredible, riveting star presence," video director Marcus Nispel said.

By 1992, a new set of Black film stars, actors, and filmmakers were moving into the mainstream. Spike Lee was adding the final touches to his big-budget biography of Malcolm X, starring Denzel Washington. Wesley Snipes, who had attracted notice in Lee's *Mo' Better Blues,* was beginning his action movie series. Wendell B. Harris won the Grand Prize at the Sundance Film Festival for producing, directing, writing, and starring in *Chameleon Street.* And, most celebrated of all was 21-year-old Los Angeles filmmaker John Singleton whose

Lisa Rose/Globe Photos

Tupac Shakur
and Rosie Perez

Boyz N the Hood had made him the youngest person ever nominated for a Best Director Academy Award. *Boyz N the Hood* had also made a movie star out of rapper Ice Cube—a signal to Tupac that hiphop's time had come. Discussing his career potential, he told Afeni, "Rappers gonna blow up out there!"

And Singleton wanted him. "When I saw *Juice*, Tupac's performances jumped out at me like a tiger. Here was an actor who could portray the ultimate crazy nigga. A brother who could embody the freedom that an 'I don't give a fuck' mentality gives a Black man. I thought this was some serious acting." With *Poetic Justice*, Singleton offered Tupac a role that would stretch his abilities to create a very different portrait of a young urban Black man, a character as recognizable and affirmative as the character Ice Cube had created in *Boyz N the Hood*. In turn, Tupac's hiphop credibility would lend Singleton the energy and authenticity he needed to distinguish his films from conventional Hollywood product. By pairing Tupac with Janet Jackson (by '91 a major entertainment figure on the basis of two breakthrough, internationally beloved albums, *Control* and *Rhythm Nation)*, Singleton hoped to create a landmark film exploding with contemporary energy, glamour, and romance. Telling a love story for the hiphop nation, Singleton chose Jackson to represent the young Black female experience and Tupac to stand in for all the righteous brothers.

Despite their high hopes, the shooting experience wasn't properly "respectful" when it came to pairing a raw gangsta upstart with a junior pop diva. "During the filming of *Poetic Justice*, 'Pac both rebelled and accepted my attitude toward him as director/advisor. This was our dance in life and work," Singleton rued. "We'd argue, then make up. Tupac spoke from a position that cannot be totally appreciated unless you understand the pathos of being a nigga, a displaced African soul, full of power, pain and passion, with no focus or direction for all that energy except his art."

After production wrapped, Tupac confirmed rumors that he had been asked to take an AIDS test:

Tupac Shakur and Janet Jackson in Poetic Justice.

It's absolutely true. I don't know if it was Janet that it came from. But I know that—suddenly out of the blue—they wanted me to take an aids test for this love scene. I didn't disagree if we were really gonna make love. I said if I can make love with Janet Jackson, I take four AIDS tests. But if I'm gonna do a love scene with her just like somebody else did—and they didn't take a test! Then I'm not takin' the test. Not only am I not taking a test, but get out of my trailer. I was like..! And they sent like four different people to ask me. First they sent the producer, then they sent the black dude, then they

sent John, then they send the girl. It don't matter who you send, I'm not takin' one, It's just to me it's an insult just to ask me that.

Problems went still deeper in Tupac's account of Jackson changing her phone number to avoid him:

It probably wasn't intentional; everybody changes their number. I mean it was so. . . I really thought I made a friend, I thought, 'I know Janet Jackson for life!' You know soon as the movie was over it was like hmm. 'This number has been changed.' And it was like a movie. I mean, it [happened] the day after the movie wrapped. The last day I saw her I saw her and Rene [Elizondo] her boyfriend, I said 'You wanna go play paint guns? We play paint guns, all right? I'm gonna call you. Alright?' 'This number has been changed.' I said, 'Wow, so ok, so it was an act.' Naw, but I think that's just. . . whatever.

By the time *Poetic Justice* was released, the most one could say for it is that it wasn't that bad. At the very least, it positioned Tupac in the spotlight his fans knew he deserved. Singleton exhibits his fondness for the politics that influences Black lives. Why else would he name his romantic couple Justice and Lucky? But, as it turns out, *Poetic Justice* is simply too forthright, too artless, and too confused to consciously employ political symbolism.

Singleton takes the subject of male-female relationships literally by using Justice, a South Central Los Angeles hairdresser, and Lucky, a young postal employee, to represent the best impulses of today's young Blacks. A perfect Hollywood romance like Vincente Minnelli's *The Clock* (1945) succeeded as a workaday fantasy, but *Poetic Justice* simply observes the common details of modern dating. Justice and Lucky spar with each other, unable to bridge the ordinary distances that make women and men wary of each other. In the movie's best, if hokiest moment, Justice, Lucky, and another bickering couple stop off at a beach. Physically aloof, their interior monologues express their isolated, bored, anxious

Tupac Shakur and Janet
Jackson in Poetic Justice.

Everett Collection

thoughts. It recalls the great beach scene in Michelangelo Antonioni's *Le Amiche* (but without Antonioni's profound sense of characters inhabiting a singular moment or going through one of life's turning points).

This separation is Singleton's central metaphor: *Poetic Justice* is about love in a time of deprivation. Justice meets Lucky while mourning her boyfriend Markell (played by Q-Tip), who was killed—significantly—at a drive-in movie (a place for escapism where there is no escape); Lucky's emotional barrier is his fouled-up parenthood (he has a daughter by a junkie) and career frustrations (he wants to be a rap artist—Singleton's foolish attempt to make rappers seem like ordinary people). These are not people who have nothing else to do but fall in love; they're desperate for the meager happiness that movie fantasy says is everyone's due.

The success of *Boyz N the Hood* proved that Singleton had a knack. Casting Tupac gave his picture a special advantage. Singleton's ability to convey the emotions that Black people identify even within stereotypes is as uncanny as Peter Bogdanovich's gift for showing the way people reach beyond their loneliness in superb films like *The Last Picture Show* and *Texasville*. *Poetic Justice* has two Bogdanovich-worthy moments: the ominous phone call Roger Guenver Smith receives in the beauty shop where he works alongside Justice and the sassy-cynical proprietor (Tyra Ferrell); and the final look of stupefied good fortune that crosses Tupac's face. Theses scenes are vivid and evocative—scenes that build a mythology whether or not the artist who made them shows depth or finesse.

Tupac Shakur and Janet Jackson in Poetic Justice.

The Kobal Collection

Poetic Justice fails at its most obvious ambitions. The bad versifying—intended to illustrate Black women's unarticulated thoughts and emotions—doesn't stand up to the wit, incisiveness, or hard, profane truth of rap lyrics. Justice and Lucky's road trip from Los Angeles to Oakland should inspire a hiphop epic in the classical sense of the term, but Justice seems as dense as Singleton in her failure to reflect on her experiences and transform them into the kind of art that might satisfy her intelligence (and enlighten the audience).

At best, Justice is a naive artist; and this is also true of Singleton, who fills out the road trip with an Afrocentric carnival, a family reunion. Instead of revealing more about the social and spiritual conditions of modern America— as done in the great seventies road movies from *Rafferty and the Gold Dust Twins* to *The Sugarland Express*—Singleton sticks to hiphop homilies and two-bit ironies. Compared to a great rap record like DJ Quik's "Jus Lyke Compton," an aural road movie contemplating the Black ways of life across the country, *Poetic Justice* didn't cut it.

Somehow Singleton made the mistake of forcing Janet Jackson into faking urban toughness when a better film might have been made of a clash between her dainty, princess sexiness running up against Tupac's bugged-out ruffneck. As it turned out in 1993, Tupac's friends-turned-nemeses, the Hughes Brothers, stole Singleton's thunder with their sensationalistic *Menace II Society*. *Poetic Justice* flopped at the box office and later at video rental counters. Singleton had proved himself capable of a wide thematic range comparable to Spike Lee's— but his style was hesitant. Tupac's idea of hiphop art was more urgent—getting right to the point.

CHAPTER 10
trials of the hiphop famous

"i want to be in a movie that don't

fuck around. That proves I can act and show something to people," Tupac declared after *Poetic Justice* failed to ignite the 'hood. He may have been speaking out of disappointment. Singleton's movie had been trumped by *Menace II Society*. Stoney was the movie role Tupac had wanted. The Hughes Brothers had ripped the story of Stoney (played by Laurenz Tate) right out of *Juice*—"I don't give a fuck" is also Stoney's signature line. Tupac's brashness inspires the movie, even though he and the Hughes Brothers couldn't come to terms on making the film together.

Relations between the filmmakers and the rapper had deteriorated over phone conversations and through business conferences that kept them at cross purposes. As happens in hiphop, insults flew like rumours, and bad blood filled the air like summer humidity. This friction had led to an altercation on the set of a Hughes Brothers music video in Los Angeles earlier that year. Tupac and his boys stormed the set to confront the Hughes Brothers. Witnesses say Tupac, swinging a baseball bat, went after each of the twins, cornering Albert Hughes while Allen fled. The throw-down wound up in court. Stories of Tupac's rage ran through Hollywood and suddenly, the only role he could get was minor—another dangerous thug in *Above the Rim*, a movie about basketball and the ghetto. Hoop nightmares.

Nov.19, 1993: Tupac Shakur is led from the Manhattan North police precinct after being arrested in an alleged sexual attack.

By the end of 1993, when Singleton was preparing production on his next movie, *Higher Learning*, executives at Columbia Pictures forced him to drop Tupac from the cast. (Ice Cube eventually played the role of an angry college student who inspires others to both protest and study Black history.) Tupac was no longer seen as just a music video or big-screen bad boy. He was for real.

That year, Tupac was hounded by trouble. On October 31, he was arrested in Atlanta for allegedly shooting at two off-duty police officers. According to Tupac, he was simply driving through the city with friends and swerved, barely missing two white women who were crossing the street; they were the wives of local policemen, brothers Mark and

Scott Whitwell. When Tupac and his friends got out of the car, one of the officers pointed a gun at the group. Gunfire followed argument. This was the kind of action that fuels the Tupac legend. As Alex Meija explains "If you get pulled over by the police, you wanna say, 'fuck the police.' But you know what, there's not a camera there while you're saying it. Here's someone in the limelight, so when he goes out there and he says 'fuck y'all,' he's voicing what everyone felt." Because he felt like firing back, Tupac was arrested, then released on $55,000 bail. The Whitwells later dropped their charges.

But the worst was yet to come, and friends saw it looming. Bay Area rapper Richie Rich was in awe:

> See, 'Pac was one of them niggas who was doing it. See, some motherfuckers'll do it, and they ain't gon' act like they doing it . . . 'Pac gon' let you know. He gon' bring the motherfuckin' money with him and the whole nine. A nigga was just real . . . he was real flamboyant, ain't nothing wrong with it when you're feelin' good.

Tupac was pushing the envelope. Even Money B recognized an escalation of the license to groove that he and Tupac had celebrated in such Digital Underground songs as the new jack valentine, "Kiss You Back" and the Playboy advisory "I Get Around." Money B sorted it out:

> You know when you go to a spot, you meet a chick . . . You be thinking, 'Damn, I want some pussy hella bad, I wonder if she gon' give me some pussy?' 'Pac would say, 'Are you gonna give me some pussy? Can I get my dick sucked right now? If I can't get my dick sucked right now, no disrespect but you gotta go, 'cause I'm gonna be tired in a little while. I gotta go and find somebody to suck my dick." And chicks would be like, 'Aw, he ain't shit,' but every nigga wanna say that, you know, every girl wanna say that, "Nigga, eat my pussy right now'. . . And that's kind like how everybody wants to be.

Back in New York City, Tupac demanded his player's rights at Nells, a hot spot for the Downtown elite who favored a Chelsea locale. Not far from the meat-packing district—a crossroads of bohemia, Eurotrash, and middle-to-no-class transience—Nell's took on a hiphop clientele as the hoi polloi moved eastward. It was a nightlife version of white flight. Ghetto heaven ruled there on November 14th when a nineteen-year-old woman caught Tupac's attention on Nell's dance floor. As Tupac set the scene: with some cajoling, she performed oral sex on him as they briefly danced. Afterward, their private party moved to Tupac's suite at the Parker Meridien Hotel where sex continued. Then, she left. The next day, she returned to the hotel. Excusing himself from his entourage, Tupac spoke to her alone. Next, she claims, his friends broke into the room and began fondling her. Tupac says he left the room, leaving his boys, who then allegedly raped her.

These allegations would stick. For Tupac, month after month became a trial. He began work on his next album, *Me Against the World*—a title that addressed the lowering clouds, the lowering boom. Between the fall of '93 and the spring of '94, Tupac's life on the road was punctuated by courtroom appearances. His personal authority was being challenged by law and society. The Shakur tribe had been here before, but the circumstances were different. The times had changed. Tupac found himself on trial for incidents centering on personal privilege rather than the defense of the peoples' rights.

"It's like they comin' to get me for whatever reason they can," he told an engineer, while laying down a track of *Me Against the World*, racing to finish against the ticking clock he heard in his head. It wasn't just official society forcing its hand. Hiphop itself seemed to be turning on Tupac when he appeared in court to answer the Hughes Brothers' battery charge. On March 10, 1994, Tupac began serving time for his assault. By the time his fifteen-day sentence ended, *Above the Rim* had opened. It featured a song "Pour a Little Liquor" that Tupac had recorded with his Thug Life group. A memorial song portraying the ritual of mourning and remembrance that b-boys do to honor lost friends, it was based on Ice Cube's pioneering "Dead Homiez," but it seemed also to be a metaphor for Tupac's own sense of despair as trouble kept him from his buddies. In this way, he dramatized being missing from action.

Few of Tupac's internal worries—the whirring thoughts of rebellion and prerogative that motivated his bold lifestyle and hard-driving raps—ever got on screen. Movies were even less successful at revealing the complexity of his personality. *Above the Rim*, his third film, was part of that series of movies exploiting the superficial image of young Black males through the sport of b-ball—a bizarre mini-genre famously typified by *Hoop Dreams*.

Screenwriter Barry Michael Cooper, one of the numerous journalists who came to prominence on the heels of hiphop, parlayed Black street pathology into a ticket to the big time. Cooper's favorite tricks include burying homoeroticism inside supposed ghetto slang—"You wanna *bount* me? You lookin' like you wanna *bount* me?"—and furthering Black criminal stereotypes. *Above the Rim* indulges easy image-mongering. Tupac plays Birdie, a devilish drug dealer who, in competition with his older, straight-arrow brother, becomes a gang leader and tries to corrupt the hood's good-guy ball players. This part could take Tupac no further in delineating urban male chaos than *Juice* already had.

Those words, said to a journalist while promoting *Above the Rim*, are more to the point of hiphop male anguish than any of the dialogue Birdie actually gets to speak. He's introduced as a cigar-chewing bad boy. His second

> I put my heart into making Birdie the evillest, meanest, wacked-out nigga. Cuz people got to know what its like to have everybody against you and you feel like bein' a killin' motherfucker who bring everybody else down if the shit don't work out right. Cuz his world ain't goin' the way it supposed to.

scene frames him in Hell-red lighting—an unintentionally funny version of the Charlie Murphy scenes in *CB4*. Tupac's determination to make an original character is sabotaged by Cooper's cliches. It's not a new turnabout but now the box office currency of hiphop endows the film with a fake legitimacy on things ghetto. To explain himself, fiendish Birdie trips to his righteous brother (Leon), "I was in a bodega with Mama's food stamps. The niggas were laughin' at me!" It's weaker than any of the motivations heard on a typical Tupac's album rant. So is Birdie's boast about buying his mother "a split-level duplex, big screen TV, marble floors."

Tupac gives these line conviction; he understands the common, hiphop era weakness for using creature comforts to measure progress. His passionate social reflexes hook into Cooper's crap. Tupac, along with Wayans (of the notorious showbiz clan) and Cooper, share the young comers' compulsion to channel the complications of their striving into simple commercial narratives even when it results in trite moralizing. The video-exploiters of *Hoop Dreams*, didn't do it any worse. The ending of *Above the Rim*, when Tupac is killed by Wayans, makes it clear that the visions of death Tupac favored were based as much in melodrama as in foresight. Tupac's Hollywood work used fantasy to reinforce his undeniable sense of dread.

In November of '94, Tupac was scheduled to stand trial in New York for the sexual assault charge at the Parker Meridien—his most serious drama yet. Undeterred, Tupac continuously wrote new raps. He began filming music videos, another creative outlet and an extension of his enterprising urge. The Shakur family dynamism spurred him on. He also contributed vocals and moral support to friends' recordings. Rapper Little Shawn asked for his help on a new track. Tupac is remembered agreeing, "I'm not letting this trial stop me. I'mo make records, I'mo make movies *anyway*!"

Entering the dank foyer of Quad Recording Studios on Seventh Ave in New York City, Tupac walked into the elevator, on his way to do a verse for the Little

Shawn session, when muggers attacked. He was shot five times; $50,000 worth of jewelry was taken off his person; repeated kicks and stomps were put to his prone body. The apparent robbery, by two men with guns, left Tupac for dead. Tupac later insisted

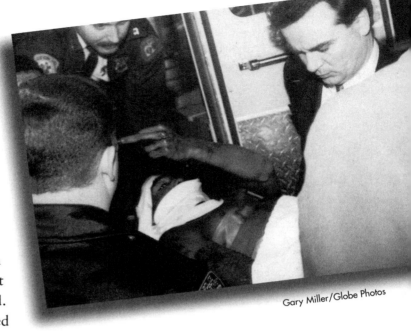

Gary Miller/Globe Photos

it was a setup stemming from a rivalry with The Notorious B.I.G., the young East Coast rapper who had been so interested in Tupac's Thug Life until industry rivalry came between them.

After a three-hour bout of surgery, Tupac made his famous overnight recovery, insisting on immediate release from the hospital. He went right back to the streets with a vengeance—and with the entire scenario of the East Coast/West Coast competition thought out and strategized. "Niggaz wanna come down hard this way, I be ready for they asses. Ain't no time to play no more!," he was quoted as saying. The shooting and robbery were never resolved, but Tupac moved on with certainty, hanging tough as the Shakur legacy had taught. Wounded, he now felt like a soldier; like a battle-scarred veteran with the glory of war in his heart. It was no longer simply a promotional ploy to sell records—the East Coast/West Coast Thang became one of many scores Tupac was determined to settle.

In court the next day, bandaged and body-weary but hell-bent on toughing

Tupac Shakur is wheeled from court in a wheelchair December 1 after making an appearance in a courtroom where he is charged with sexual molestation.

it out, Tupac was acquitted of sodomy and weapons charges but found guilty of sexual abuse. (Tupac's associate, Charles Fuller, acknowledged having oral sex with the woman but insisted it was consensual.) Tupac was sent to Riker's Island where he faced an 18-month to four-and-a-half year sentence. Jail is where the Panther and hiphop legacies would do a karmic face-off. Tupac began serving time on Valentine's Day 1995.

CHAPTER 11
word is bondage

me against the world opens with a

mock radio news summary of Tupac's recent troubles:

> At 12:25 a.m. Wednesday Tupac was on his way into a Times
> Square building to record at an 8th floor studio with
> another rapper. But in the lobby Tupac was shot several
> times. including two graze wounds to the head. Tupac's
> lawyers said the attack appeared to be a set-up.

In self-mythologizing, Tupac recognized the scope of his life and career. After so much courtroom, hospital, and big-screen bravado, his third album *(Me Against the World)* hit the street (debuting at Number One on Billboard's pop chart) while he was still incarcerated. It carried a double message of the "political prisoner"copping a plea, like a caught rat—okay, a distressed child. That's what he is at heart—despite hiphop's macho affectations. Listeners who might otherwise be outraged, or confused by Tupac's tendency to talk out of both sides of his mouth can hear the poignancy in his voice and respond to his rock-bottom vulnerability.

So much sentimentality is etched into *Me Against the World,* it resembles a tombstone. In the title track, a female backing vocalist (Dramacyde—a surefire touch in the style of Dr. Dre) provides the song's formulaic basis. Ghetto cynicism is stated then romanticized in contrasting male/female voices, with Tupac imitating lines made famous on "Ghetto Bastard" by Naughty by Nature's Treach: "I got nothing to lose," he boasts—but for a successful professional musician, it's a lie.

Tupac's stance first seduces, then insults those brothers who listen to him but never had the benefit of his talents or his opportunities. This could be taken as a sign of pop's rich ability to bypass logic for the emotional connection, yet it is also the basis of Tupac's moral complexity—and his betrayal of both himself and his audience. Atron Gregory, his first producer, had Tupac's complicated image figured out:

> **A lot of people would like to say Tupac changed, but most people didn't know him. Plus, they only knew him from 1993 to now. You know, whatever, they may say he changed, but they didn't know where he came from or what he was all about. He was always about doing what he had to do to make it to the top of his career.**

When listeners identify with the little bit of sense and humanity in Tupac's raps, their response is reduced to accepting the role he crafted in the studio as an expression of his personal and political turmoil. As sold by the record industry, Tupac's compassion became a form of middlebrow moralizing—a distraction from the balanced thoughts and difficulty of honest, integral living.

On "So Many Tears"—an R&B lament designed for adolescent hearts—Tupac says "I'm having visions of leaving here in a hearse," just like the rest of us. Yet, it's shrewdly commercial; he's also ripping-off the Geto Boys' lavishly morbid rap tunes. He leaves out his real life bad behavior that draws the hearse near, the toughness that would make his macabre verses abrasive and interesting. On the album's next cut he grovels: "Even thugs get lonely." It's not a good enough line to move any but the most simpleminded; they can only relate to the sappy teenage subtext of being misunderstood. Tupac's con is exposed by the song's title, "Temptations." It's a hood's wink.

Terrible thing is, when Tupac puts himself on the witness stand, you can't trust the appraisal of his own experience. "Young Niggaz" ought to be autobiographical but, dedicated to kids trying to be gangstas, it uses a bogus *Menace II Society, Sugar Hill* narrative. Tupac appeals to the cliché rather than truth, encouraging young people to see themselves as stereotypes, not individuals. The song's list of social disasters is not a political alarm. And when Tupac offers advice: "You could be a fuckin' accountant not a dope dealer; you could be a lawyer," he gives away a quick-fix alternative that sounds suspiciously close to his own yuppie/jailbird worries. If Tupac is sincere about reform, why does the album end up with "Outlaw" encouraging eleven- year-old kids to gangbang?

Full of moral inconsistencies, Tupac raps: "I woke up and screamed 'Fuck the world!'" But his curse has no target, no purpose, no wit; it's bullshit. So is "It Ain't Easy." Appealing to the myth of himself and Mike Tyson as political heroes without ethical responsibilities, Tupac gives a shout-out to Tyson:

Sometimes the personal is political; but sometimes the personal is simply narcissistic and self-involved. The only

"I'ma hold your hand and holler 'THUG LIFE!'. . .
It ain't easy being me
will I see the penitentiary
Or will I stay free?"

album track that wouldn't make George Jackson, Nelson Mandela, and Geronimo Pratt retch is the booty ballad "Can U Get Away," featuring Tupac's romanticism and seduction unsullied by pretense.

When Tupac blurts out: "I'm just a young Black man cursed since birth," on "Heavy in the Game," he gets it completely wrong and makes a terrible game out of the pitfalls of racism. "Death Around the Corner"'s use of "gallows wisdom" (which some have taken to be prophetic) actually shows Tupac to be blessed by the music industry. He's the perfect product of an exploitative/destructive system. No matter how many promote Tupac as a symbol of Black male struggle, the female chorus on "Heavy in the Game" (voices of mother-wit) delivers the mercenary entertainer's true, narcissistic epitaph: "*I don't care what it did to them, [the] game's been good to me.*" Tupac leans against a wall on the album cover of *Me Against the World*—a sepia silhouette. It's a glamour shot that transforms his eccentricity into matinee idol mystery.

After *Me Against the World*, Tupac's mounting legal battles began to look like a public performance. More and more frequently, his name made it into the news. He was hit by the ricochet effect of pop art when that teen who killed a Texas state trooper claimed *2pacalypse Now* had inspired him to do it. "Pac told me to" became the excuse of young men caught in that strange, frustrated limbo between fantasy and realty. Equally roguish politicians picked it up and used it to gain political mileage. Both those reactions scapegoated rap culture; the surface motive for a widening gulf between cops and the unempowered, adults and youth, art and the law.

All this notoriety lifted Tupac out of the mean anonymity of ghetto crime into the celebrity mystique and status that hiphop has codified as "gangsta." It wasn't always the establishment press that turned a troubled life into entertainment. dream hampton, a lower-case pop writer, wrote a Tupac "journal" for the white-owned hiphop magazine, *The Source,* that traded on egregious trivializations of Tupac's travails. She begins her article, "Hellraiser," by recounting her dream of a Tupac tantrum:

There's a purity to Tupac's rage. Yes, he's dangerously emotional, but right-eously so. He believes something and is willing to act on it. For him conformi-ty means the death of truth. We plea for him to return to the car but he has already pimped his way into the darkness.

Ascribing "Godly quality" to his voice, hampton recalls Tupac jiving with buddies in a recording studio with his "big beautiful infectious laugh, and all is forgiven." Her suck-up continues with a report on Tupac's 1994 trial for assaulting the Hughes brothers. "Tupac strolls in twenty minutes [after the Hugheses] with the completed tracks from last night's [recording session] blast-ing in his headphones." When a hallway scuffle takes place between Tupac and Allen Hughes, who taunts "Aww, you l'il bitch! Put 'em up!," hampton gets off her most imaginative line: "Tupac's heart asks his ears for a soundcheck. Still, he's not at a loss for words."

Lisa Rose/Globe Photos

Tupac Shakur at LA Municipal Court to face 15 days jail for assault and battery on Film Director Allan Hughes.

This kind of mythmaking turns the courthouse experience into a farce. It appeals to the capricious attitude of the hiphop marketplace that inspires fans to take legal dilemmas lightly. Useless exploitation of rebellion is rebellion for the hell of it; false bravado is encouraged in place of reason and sober reflection. Hampton perverts the desperate dynamic of most inner city courtroom trials that center around Black intramural crimes and grievances.

Of all the criminal charges against him, Tupac admitted that the Hughes Brothers case is "the only one I'm really guilty of"—a more honest statement than most of what appears on *Me Against the World*. But hampton twists an absurd justification out of this:

> There's an unspoken law in our community that two Black men should never be in court for battery. They should avoid fighting when possible and, when they do it, it should be fair and not fatal. Someone loses, someone wins. there may be retaliation. In worst case scenarios, it may escalate into full blown violence and neighborhood wars, but never should it be taken to the police.

This is nonsense. Criminally stupid. By these standards, hampton would have to agree that witnesses to Tupac's shooting should keep silent and protect the killers. Such journalism is a nightmare of cultural propaganda, not a dream. (The thought of hampton, allegedly the niece of slain Black Panther Fred Hampton, raising a kid—and singing him Nas lyrics as lullabies, she revealed in *The Village Voice*—is ghastly. Calling Tupac "the most beautiful rapper alive, " she confuses her own fan hysteria with Black political imperative. Her "Hellraiser" article cheapens the sad truth of what happens to mismotivated rebellion. hampton's misunderstanding of the legal restrictions Black youth encounter leads her to pretend a shallow appreciation of what has become a common American sorrow in an era of cyclical crime bills designed to corral social misfits. To treat Tupac's troubles as entertainment shows a lack of genuine sympathy. It's the worst kind of hiphop mythmaking because it's bereft of pity.

Wiser feminine instincts are voiced in YoYo's single "Letter to the Pen," where she transforms "Nuthin but a G Thang" from its original celebration of ghetto cruelty to a hard-edged expression of a woman's loyalty. In writing to her incarcerated lover, her words of comfort contrast the maddening compulsions, the negative forces that make life hellish for young Black males. YoYo turns a regular love letter into a defensive weapon. She counters "the system" (referring to her political prisoner loved one as "soldier"—an arguable endearment) but, most significantly, she defies male self-destruction by offering a woman's vote of confidence. "Letter to the Pen" opens up a story most hiphop songs ignore— knowing a convict personally has become commonplace in modern America. It takes a down sister to speak to the forgotten men of the hiphop era—those who pay the less dramatic, dreadful, wearying price for bangin' and mackin'. This is a challenge to the reckless bravado of superficial male rappers and bogus rap journalists.

Me Against the World works out Tupac's memory of strife through imaginatively representing his recent crises—the November '93 indictment on charges that he and some associates had sodomized a nineteen-year-old woman in a Manhattan hotel suite. His comeuppance soon after: he was shot five times, and robbed of $50,000 in jewelry. This was followed by his eventual conviction on first-degree sexual abuse charges. By June '96 he had pending sentences for probation violations in New York and Los Angeles. And yet, it's important to remember, *people loved Tupac*—women, in particular, still think of him knowingly and forgivingly, with the kind of devotion matched only by their dedication to Luther Vandross and Michael Jackson. They empathize and feel protective toward the young man the world is against. And much of this love centers on one magnificently complex song.

CHAPTER 12
dear mama

"dear mama,"

a tribute to his mother, determined how Tupac would forever be regarded by fans. The main reason *Me Against the World* racked up double-platinum sales, "Dear Mama" makes hiphop sense. It displays the heart and sensitivity behind a music mostly known for insolence. Tupac may have been serving time for sexual assault on a Black woman, but "Dear Mama," like 1993's "Keep Your Head Up," made up for it in the minds of his most ardent listeners. If this wasn't atonement, it was still deep feeling—and in the right direction. While Mike Tyson's rape conviction divided many Black Americans, Tupac's song penetrated even feminist defenses through its evocation of a life lived within the grace of a woman's love. Compared to this testament, an infraction with a nightclub skeezer seemed forgivable, indeed.

Both men and women related to the story of family striving and maternal sacrifice Tupac delivered. Slowing his pace to pay proper respect, Tupac made this his most clearly enunciated rap. His memories of growing up seem equally vivid and precise, each detail substantiating the elements of a universal Black American childhood:

> ME AND MY MAMA HAD BEEFS
> 17 YEARS OLD
> KICKED OUT ON THE STREETS
> THOUGH BACK AT THE TIME
> I NEVER THOUGHT I'D SEE HER FACE
> AIN'T A WOMAN ALIVE
> THAT CAN TAKE MY MAMA'S PLACE

Tupac puts his childhood ignorance alongside his present understanding, placing "Dear Mama" in the greatest tradition of American folk songs. Yet, because hiphop's revelations are based in social anguish, even the simplest emotions are complicated.

Put all Afeni's qualities together—activism, passion, affection, enthusiasm, neurosis, independence—and they spell an original kind of motherhood. That's an intimate subject for a young recording artist. In "Dear Mama" Tupac explored it in the style of those folk songs that touch on a spiritual regard for parenthood and social struggle. This gentle song is, at long last, the answer to the cynicism of "Smilin' Faces (Sometimes)" that a politically conscious boy owed to the mother who brought him up—and through. "Dear Mama" is distinguished by personal details reflecting Black social struggle and oppression.

But Tupac's celebration and testimony are not specific to the affection Black children feel for their mothers, nor are they an unusual expression of badboy remorse. Merle Haggard got there first with his 1972 classic, "Mama Tried." It's unlikely that Tupac heard or knew of this white artist or his Country-

Western song well enough to append his own version—but the similarities between "Dear Mama" and "Mama Tried" are great pop serendipity.

Haggard, from a poor Oklahoma family, spent most of his teenage years in reformatories for petty crimes. "Mama Tried," written in 1968, recalls Haggard's imprisonment in San Quentin at age nineteen, convicted of armed robbery. The songs are alike in dealing with adoration and repentance. The image and influence of mother prevails over each man's sense of himself, limiting the boastful bullshit almost as though an approving/disproving eye were watching over them in the recording studio. Both Tupac and Haggard show what it's like for a rebel to feel humbled. Their abashment contradicts the hell-raiser image of both country and hiphop music; it keeps one mindful that the hand that rocks the cradle can rock the conscience of those who rock the world.

But it's the distinctions separating these songs that reveal each performer's personality and the differences separating the cultural traditions and social outlooks they come from. "Dear Mama" so deeply pierces the heart of Black American sentimentality that a listen to Haggard's version of family love works as a corrective. While Tupac constructs his sentimental autobiography, he bases it on an ode to the woman who raised him; he omits a reality check on the self-indulgent narrator.

I ain't guilty
Cuz even though I sell rocks
It feels good puttin' money in your mail box

This is a remarkable piece of absolution—the ghetto's drug plague (and Tupac's part in it as a crack dealer in Marin City) described from the point of desperation *plus* generosity. Swooning to this song involves recognizing that people sell drugs out of necessity more than meanness. In this view, gangbanging becomes a search for affection rather than a descent into violence.

Tupac offers amnesty to those who feel swamped by other peoples' judgments. Indeed, the personal pleading in "Dear Mama" allows the bad child within every listener to do that popular nineties thing—forgive themselves. It's a short cut to the atonement later sought in the Million Man March; Tupac probably affected just as many people by leading them along the sentimental path.

Hiphop's tendency to prize passion over cool and cool over truth, is an aberration of American pop expression. Willing to exchange tall-tale sentiment for self-examination, a hiphop artist can romanticize both his mama and his dreams of freedom in ways that can only lead only to confusion.

Haggard avoided this trap because country music has a more candid relationship to its audience. "Mama Tried" is a frank admission of guilt:

```
            I turned 21 in prison
            Doing life without parole
No one could steer me right but Mama tried.
        Mama tried to raise me better
        But her pleadin' I denied
        That leaves only me to blame
            'Cuz Mama tried.
```

Haggard's mama tried to represent the law to him as an uncontestable force—a standard to be respected, obeyed, but above all, loved. You can see the changes in cultural and industry practices in the mama-love song that complements Haggard's—Dolly Parton's 1971 "Coat of Many Colors." In those days, Parton was a recognizably serious artist (as guileless and innocent as Iris DeMent). The folk-pop artist's mandate was to speak from the heart, unashamedly, about the virtues of struggle inside poverty. "Coat of Many Colors" was powerful because the singer's sentimental regard for her mother's handiwork also exposed the hell of poverty. Parton sang autobiographically of the outside world's cruelty. The ridicule of her derisive schoolmates made her suffer the indignities of class, leaving a wound that was so close to the poignance of love that the two are mixed unforgettably—and almost unforgivably. (*"One is only poor/ Only if they choose to be."*) Parton's personal politics help explain her determined showbiz climb, but they also represent qualities of integrity that developing folk genres seem to lose over time.

Haggard turned Parton's motherlove around. While making sense of his own hardships, he created a picture of a society more just than Parton's, manfully heaping blame upon himself—an America-first attitude, less insightful than Parton's humanism and the flipside of Tupac's cynicism. There is something correct in Haggard's self-criticism, but it's also somewhat deluded in the way he measures social standards against his own instincts. Hiphop artists do this too, but come up with a different judgement because they know that society's moral standards are, first of all, arbitrary and inequitable.

As Parton's mother represented God's grace and providence; and Tupac's mother, the prevailing Black sojourner; Haggard's mother embodied his love for America. In "Mama Tried," he testifies to an ex-con's chastened allegiance. It's not a parole board hoax, the mama metaphor is there—and it is stirring—because he's sincere.

Haggard's career demonstrates a political alternative to hiphop. "Mama Tried" is different from "Dear Mama" not merely because of race or trite urban vs. rural notions; it represents a difference in time and in the effects that history has had on social consciousness, turning indigenous patriots into homegrown cynics. You can best understand this generational difference by considering the changes in American ideology that, in the seventies, made a patriotic doily-waver out of a Haggard motherfucker and, in the nineties, turned Tupac, an unrepentent fuck-up, into a motherlover.

Country-western conservatism has much to do with social complacency (*"From a family meek and mild,"* "Mama Tried" begins) and that's what you get in the scoffing, belligerent condemnations of Haggard's "The Fightin' Side of Me," "Workingman Blues," and "Okie from Muskogee." Despite the counterculture's espousal of new ways to think about government and morality, conservative artists, rakes, and taxpayers reacted with fright and tenacity—a colorfully spoken, culturally authentic stubbornness. You hear the specters of both the civil rights movement and the Vietnam war protests behind Haggard's songs; his jingoism covers up his disappointment in the very things his non-political hell-raising protested against. Haggard, like many late-awakening Americans, did not connect his private misery to politics. A callused political disaffection readied him for a fight, spurring him to defy petty laws while traditionally respecting larger rules.

"Even though you was a crack fiend, Mama You still was a Black queen, Mama."

In "Hungry Eyes," the underbelly to "Mama Tried," Haggard laments *"Mama never had the luxury she wanted/ And it wasn't 'cause my Daddy didn't try."* The sense of futility here aches; the patriot who sings those lines must also squirm. The hardship that makes for "Hungry Eyes"—an image of exquisite deprivation to go with the sad, twangy melody—sounds so rooted. Pure country artists like Haggard respond to a long legacy of desperation: *"Another class of people/ Put us somewhere just below."* This song, a memory of life in a canvas-covered labor camp shack, delineates class conflict without explicitly questioning it. Its terror is in the opening line of "Mama Tried:" *"First thing I remember knowin'/ Was a lonesome whistle blowin.'"* It gives a clear sense of a people isolated by poverty and mired in ignorance with its attendant mythology of working-class virtue.

Haggard's self-righteousness reveals that he missed out on the good sense of protest that the civil rights movement fomented, not just in Black people but in the conclaves of women, intelellectuals, artists, bohemians, and gays. It also means that generations later, rappers like Tupac—the ghetto bastards of campus radicals—would have no trouble claiming their right to object to a system of deprivation, to scowl with hungry eyes.

Watching his own mother's suffering, Tupac would pen "Dear Mama's" most difficult line unburdened by Haggard's sense of social conflict. *"Even though you was a crack fiend, Mama/ You still was a Black queen, Mama."* In response to his rock-cocaine-addicted mother, Tupac voiced a sorrier circumstance than Haggard could even imagine.

Rap sophistication includes the awareness of what poverty and social inequity does to people—and speaks out about it more boldly than conservative country-western. And though the reasons for this may also be racial, they derive particularly from a contrasting sense of rap's wounded entitlement and country-western's grim forebearance. In the two decades separating "Mama Tried" from "Dear Mama," those polar attitudes have come together in a national, cross-cultural malaise.

Nowhere was this more disturbingly demonstrated than when Afeni Shakur appeared on a network interview show to decry Death Row Records' swindling of Tupac's supposed fortune.

Please remember that my great grandmother was a slave, my grandmother was a sharecropper, my mother was factory worker and I was a legal worker. Do you understand? So this represents the first time in our life, in our memory ever, that we have been able to enjoy the American dream, and that's what Tupac brought to his family.

Afeni's words echo the grandmother's speech from A *Raisin in the Sun,* then get down to harsh reality:

I discovered that Tupac had next to zero, next to nothing. I discovered that the

home that he had just bought was not his. Let's say that the entertainment business is a business of prostitution and thievery and that it was rampant around my son. I simply feel that I have a responsibility to my son, whom I carried in my womb, and that has nothing to do with Suge Knight or anyone. That has only to do with Tupac Shakur and Afeni Shakur.

Facing up to Afeni's qualities, Detroit journalist Emma Lockridge has observed the effects of this tragic spiritual merger. "I've been haunted by him. Tupac's death to me is the failure of our generation because we're the ones who spawned him. His mother was so full of rage that she finally let this system chew her up and spit her out." Afeni could initiate and quit social options before her children's own hungry eyes. But her all-too-human travail is reflected in Tupac's contradictions. Unlike Haggard, Tupac witnessed not only his mother's hunger, but also her faithlessness, and her proud Panther spirit broken. His art expresses a deep loss, a greater sense of dislocation than Haggard's rueful banditry. But utter confusion intrudes upon the sentiments of "Dear Mama" whether or not listeners choose to hear it.

Tupac could never have covered "Mama Tried" because its sense of trust— its optimism—would have seemed naive and totally foreign to him. So "Dear Mama" gainsays any real sense of Tupac's responsibility, offering, instead, self-condemnation in favor of her heroism, exploiting the most shameless sentimentality in Black pop music. Because of "Dear Mama," *Me Against the World* stayed at Number One on the album sales charts for three weeks, anticipating Mother's Day, until Ice Cube's *Friday* soundtrack rightfully took over the top spot.

"Dear Mama" pours treacle in Black culture's bloodstream and thins the remorse in hiphop ferocity. When Tupac raps about hell in "Lord Knows," directing his mawkishness (*"If you can make it through the night, there's a better day"*) to the world of sin, failure, and regret, he's asking for pity.

In "Dear Mama's" melody line, Tupac updates "Sadie," The Spinners' great ode to mothers. The song's basic truth is that mamalove lives in Black American culture even past absurdity. It may seem cruel to claim that such affection is ridiculous; certainly, Tupac's fans represent a value of loving in their response. But let's be plain, their emotions confer upon the record a virtue that it doesn't honestly possess.

The extreme "crack fiend/ Black queen" lyric uses the hard truth facilely (even the rhyme is fatuous, building on wacko Afrocentricity as the only tribute at hand). Absolution is the secret to the song's success, but by ignoring (forgiving) his mother's failure, Tupac also avoids understanding her complexity. He's still looking up, like a child. His best tribute *("You never kept a secret/ Always stayed real")* is a pretty strong acknowledgment of a parent's commitment to truth, yet it wilts when it could have soared by leading to a hard-learned Oedipal or social truth, perhaps detailing Afeni's advice on women, men, revolution. Instead, pathos triumphs.

CHAPTER 13 temptations

in prison, tupac told visitors that when he wanted to achieve something, he would find a picture of the thing or draw a picture. Then he would put this picture on the wall over his bed—and stare at it long and often. He would not sleep in the bed until he had achieved his goal.

What could he have been thinking those eight months on Riker's Island that turned him so impatient and ruthless?

Away from the limelight, Tupac grew restless and discontent. "When people tell him how much that record, 'Dear Mama,' means to them, he seems to get a charge out of it," a prison guard told a *New York Post* gossip columnist. Having a hit record on the charts while doing lockdown forced Tupac to examine the effect his career was having on others as well as himself. Despite a growing sense of desperation that his visitors could sense, he'd make a good will gesture now and then. When one of the guards spoke of a family tragedy, Tupac arranged to get the officer tickets to a Stevie Wonder concert, planning with a record company friend to get the tickets and present them as a surprise gift. But at other times, the odd mix of notoriety and isolation got to him. In Riker's Island's private, steel-enclosed visiting room, Tupac complained to visitors that he was being mistreated or, when depressed, protested his innocence on the sexual assault charges and expressed anger at the system that now had him "pinned" just like Mutulu and Assata. A visit from Madonna didn't mean much; the good vibes of a hit single rarely made it past prison security.

Early in his sentence, after "Dear Mama" had given him cachet as a thug with a good heart, Tupac conferred with Rev. Daughtry, who had made it a mission to pay weekly visits. Tupac wanted advice about his next step—which single to release as a follow-up. "I felt particularly elated," Daughtry said. "He asked me my opinion. He described what the records were about. I then gave him my opinion. That is the decision he made."

"*Temptations*," the next single, was a variation on "I Get Around"'s sexboast, but as Tupac explained it to Rev. Daughtry, he added a veil of piety and contrition to the song's ripe tale of worldly excess.

```
And even though I'm known for my one night stand
        I want to be an honest man
        But Temptations on me."
```

It was a shrewd move, resurrecting the randy, pre-"Dear Mama" image while inching toward redemption.

Proof that Tupac was held in great esteem by the rap community came with the video of "*Temptations*", which featured various hiphop stars appearing in support of the jailed rapper, endorsing in mime the events that had led to his incarceration. Tupac couldn't get out of jail to film a video for the single so they appeared in his stead, acting out a drama of mischief along the lines of the frolics that had been his undoing. Black outlawry occurs in nearly every frame. Tupac's voice-over rap narrates the various ways Black folks get tempted to give in to their lowest instincts. *Temptations* presents these instincts as basically sexual, accepting the racist view that Black instinct—Black sexuality—is innately lowdown. This isn't radical; it reinforces stereotype.

Like a lot of the videos MTV picked up for heavy rotation, *Temptations* showcases Black (mis)behavior for the enjoyment of voyeurs. Voyeurism is also its premise. Ice-T plays a hotel proprietor and Coolio, the bellboy who has to make a delivery to one of the guests. While pushing a tray down a hotel hallway, Coolio notices guests conspicuously slipping into their rooms. He peeps through the keyholes and we are privileged to view the obscene:

- Treach pouring honey on a hottie
- Shock G from Digital Underground looking for some
- Salt and Spinderella playing strip poke-her (a reference to TLC's Red Light Special)
- Crystal Waters with a male stripper
- Warren G with money in an attaché case later rolling with a babe in the lucre
- Jada Pinkett as an exhibitionist winking at Coolio
- Isaac Hayes waiting his turn with her
- Bill Bellamy wriggling his toes while getting serviced and videotaping the action

A seventies pop artist, describing the mystery dance of sex asked, "What's the use of looking when you don't know what [it] means?" The same question applies to *Temptations*, a treatise on Black solidarity as well as a pseudo-investigation into the troubles that arise from fornication. Video director Lionel Martin first reminds viewers of the freaky bellboy and hotel from *Barton Fink*, but the "weirdness" on view (including some bondage and lesbians in a tub) and the evident artifice of performing and spying also recall the hallway sequence in the *l'Hotel des Folies Dramatiques* in Jean Cocteau's *The Blood of a Poet*. *Temptations* similarly takes us through the looking glass of Black identity only to settle for the fetishistic images of criminal behavior that belong to an outsider's imagination. Celebrating Black sexuality without social context, the performers mime Tupac's misbehavior. Jerry Lewis's 1961 film *Ladies' Man* featured the cross-sectional view of a female dormitory designed to reveal different aspects of masculine ego and desire. Each female resident tested Lewis's evolving manhood. The makers of *Temptations* call up memories of *Ladies' Man,* but their images don't question Tupac's very questionable behavior. Only Ice-T's final dialogue, *"So long, 'snack pack,' 'back pack,' 'tube sock,' whatever,"* seems at all satirical. The rest is simple hiphop porncorn.

Temptations, like other Tupac videos, has more cinematic appeal than his first three movies yet it panders to the audience and cheapens his pop tragedy, wasting the blood of a rapper. In *Temptations*, the obscene is seen without understanding—one of the typical ways in which hiphop remains immature.

Temptations mocks the fact of Tupac's punishment. The image of him in jail recalls another like image in the *Papa'z Song* video in which Tupac avenges himself against an absentee-now-jailbird father, touching raw nerves of primal resentment in the hiphop audience. As confusing as *Temptations* is, it actually celebrates the very same male prerogatives that lead to absentee-jailbird fathers. These are not signs that he *overstands* (in Saniyka Shakur's words) the complexity of anyone's all-too-human behavior. Young fans who have not sorted out their own complex feelings about present or absent parents may feel that Tupac has only enhanced their distress. *Papa'z Song,* a star vehicle, is bogusly gratifying, which is the way of hiphop cant: Rap artists seize the kind of truth-telling opportunities that previous Black artists could only dream about (From hiphop's prehistory: Sammy Davis, Jr's autobiography *Yes, I Can* gives a good account) only to lose the moment to commercial gimmickry. Tupac's real-life thug life had become old news, but the video sticks to the surface of his suffering and the ideals he was searching for. Turning his own precious imperatives into commodities, Tupac was, indeed, playing a crap game.

Paranoia struck deep at Riker's Island. So did confusion. Tupac told Rev. Daughtry he wanted to marry Jada Pinkett, his friend from Baltimore's School of the Arts, seeing wedlock as a relief and distraction from jailhouse horrors. "He had it all planned," Daughtry said. "He wanted me to do the ceremony. The wedding would be in Atlanta." But in April, Tupac suddenly married Keisha Morris, a longtime girlfriend, in a ceremony at the Clinton Correctional Facility. The marriage was later annulled. As Tupac stewed in his cell, he obsessed on past grievances. In a *Vibe* magazine interview, he renounced his Thug Life persona, and contemplated turning over a new leaf. Then in an abrupt turnabout, he

Tupac Shakur and Jada Pinkett.

Tom Rodriguez/Globe Photos

"This type of ShIt It happeNs eVery day"

implicated The Notorious B.I.G., Puffy Combs, Andre Harrell and others in his 1994 recording studio ambush.

Jail fucked with Tupac's head. Play Slick Rick's *Behind Bars* immediately after *Me Against the World* and the difference is like graduating from nursery school to the college of hard knocks. No stranger to the docket, Ricky Walters doesn't sentimentalize the tough life that got him into jail; he just pours out the beautiful wisdom of lessons learned. *Behind Bars* (Slick Rick's third album, the first recorded entirely while in custody—a music industry first) is nothing so banal as an apologia or even a nightmare prison scenario. Rick has done some deep thinking about the troubles of living in this difficult world. His extraordinary lyrical gifts twist the puzzles, disasters, wonderings together with defiant wit.

Rick's intricate, speedy delivery, his verbal and literary skills create a brand new thrill of thinking from the gut. The title track's refrain (*"This type of shit/ It happens every day"*) intensifies rap lingo and poetic expression, making the two nearly inseparable: *"Hold my head and drift/Assume awaitin's knots and cars/Instead of sittin' here accumulatin'/Cuts and scars/Behind bars . . . "* Rick's experience of deprivation, anguish, and fear retains its trauma as the song admits his bad behavior and hidden remorse. *"Back in population/Didn't matter that his friends tense/The phone privs, the years added to the sentence/ And I escape when I dreamt/ Think so?/ I hit the cell because they made a rape attempt."* He zeroes in on the emotional constraints people face, looking outside himself to articulate the unacknowledged suffering of men and women who don't fit the stereotype.

"Behind Bars" carries a listener all the way through the fright of prison to an intricate picture of the way a scandalized mind ticks. Rapping at the speed of thought, Rick exactly conveys how hard-thinking works. "*This type of shit/It happens every day*" makes a remarkable chorus, refusing, as it does, a sentimentalization of his troubles. It's a simple but profound awareness Tupac never arrived at.

During Tupac's incarceration, hiphop went through important ethical and stylistic shifts; changes that created the East/West differences alienated Tupac who, for the moment, was not actively participating. Locked away, he resented what his nemeses, the Hughes Brothers, had done to his family's legacy in their movie, *Dead Presidents*. "Those punks are suckers. Suckers. They don't know anything about the movement, about my Auntie (Assata), they just running a game!" he railed. *Dead Presidents* sensationalized the Shakur family's political disillusionment in a flashy, superficial way that made Tupac feel ripped-off once again.

Trying to come to grips with the temptations of the music industry, trying to make sense of work by other hiphop artists that pleased or irritated him, Tupac stood at a pivotal point.

The Rebel of the Underground, the instigator of Thug Life, faced Rev. Daughtry each week and heard tell of rap acquaintances putting new moves on the scene. He felt doubt and shame for the ideas that had first motivated him. A visitor recalls Tupac's fears about being left out and left behind: "I need to get out of here and set things up so I move on these clowns. Rap is stronger now than it ever was, I can't be missin' it. I got something to say to young brothers. Biggie and 'em be blowin' up—and they got wack ideas. I know enough now to go into hiphop with some mad shit." A friend of Keisha Morris remembers, "Jail was so bad for him. It got to the point that every time 'Pac heard of some new rap star or picked up on a joint like "Flava in Your Ear" or "Doggy Dogg World," he was wanting to break out."

CHAPTER 14
in love with gangstas

"IS IT DRE? IS IT DRE?
THAT'S WHAT THEY SAY EVERYDAY IN L.A."
—"F——With Dre Day"

it was time for tupac to reassess his life.

After the all-but-deadly ambush in 1994, he had pulled his physical and mental resources together in a sort of miraculous, myth-making self-resurrection. Acquitted on sodomy and weapons charges, he still faced the guilty conviction and a sentence for sexual abuse. In jail, he had seen his third album climb the sales charts, then watched the world of hiphop spin away from him. New artists were on the rise in '95, stealing the hiphop moment. Tupac cried "bullshit" from his jail cell when he first heard people praising Snoop Doggy Dogg and The Notorious B.I.G., but later, he had to admit to Dr. Dre, producer of Snoop's hit solo album, "It's dope."

The recycled funk of slippery-voiced Snoop and the extraordinarily adept Dr. Dre sounded great to Tupac. The poisonous depiction of ghetto life on *Doggystyle* appealed to a young rap star locked away and deprived of street life with all its swaggering fantasies. Tupac must have felt a jailbird's nostalgia that paralleled the dreams of freedom and empowerment entertained by kids trapped in the 'hood. *Doggystyle* further refined the formula already "perfected" on Dre's, *The Chronic,* in its gangsta-as-hustler lore. It was a formula that took full advantage of hiphop's growing popularity among mainstream listeners hungry for Black fantasies as a clue to the other America.

Tupac now looked to gangsta rap—the L.A.Bloods, Crips, and Crisis version of hiphop—with envious eyes, realizing that those new beats were hyping up a revolution without him. Since N.W.A., Los Angeles rappers had combined anger and injustice with crude, personal appetite. At first, Tupac resented the new sound, but he came to crave the wild response it provoked. There was no denying its popularity. And, although almost a year would pass before he was out of jail and free to make his own moves, he desperately wanted in.

Revolutionaries compete with pop stars in hiphop's role model sweepstakes. The lyrics *"Is it Dre? Is it Dre? That's what they say everyday in L.A."* from Andre Young's second hit single, "F—Wit Dre Day," were a proclamation of fame, success, and acclaim; even in jail it must have struck Tupac as one of the highpoints of contemporary pop, a climax of hiphop possibility. Imperious lyrics rapped to a sinuous groove trumpeted something that Dre had made happen—an example of what Tupac, himself, wanted to achieve.

Dr. Dre at the Second Annual Source Hip Hop Music Awards on Aug. 3, 1995.

The simplest dreams of rap success that began with the first bulk sales of Sugarhill Gang's "Rapper's Delight" in 1979 were hugely confirmed by 1993, the year Dre's album *The Chronic* broke through and changed rap's politics and aesthetics. More money and media attention flowed toward hopeful ghetto talent. A portion of Hollywood excitement, once reserved exclusively for movie stars, was now available for status-craving rappers. Dre, an original member of the Los Angeles rap group N.W.A., had studied and achieved an expert command of R&B orchestration. A deft rapper as well as an imaginative producer, he had proved himself capable of using a funkadelic thump and a purely idiosyncratic synthesizer whine to convey new styles of being—of living large in the moment.

Dre's hometown appeal went nationwide. The success that *The Chronic* brought to Death Row Records—the company Dre began with Marion "Suge" Knight after the split-up of N.W.A.—became an emblem of potential that beckoned to Tupac, who now wanted his own "F——Wit 'Pac Day."

Doggystyle, Snoop's "solo" debut album—featuring Tha Dogg Pound and many of the cellmates/artists now signed to Death Row—had matched Tupac's previous feat by entering national sales charts in the Number One position—a first for a Black debut artist and an amazing example of hiphop crossover. For all the inside slang and territorial focus used by Dr. Dre and Snoop, *Doggystyle* was clearly made with a mainstream record-buying public in mind. Snoop and Dre had obviously strategized their depictions of hokey street drama (" For All My Niggaz & Bitches," "Gin and Juice"), silly, sexist aggression ("Ain't No Fun") and lame acts of violence ("Murder Was the Case") to appeal to the usual thrill-hungry teens as well as a larger audience of eager, non-thinking consumers. A mainstream critic advised readers to "buy-play-burn" this "great record." But *Doggystyle* isn't a great record and the worst thing about a hiphop crossover act is that it allows listeners from the non-core audience to disregard hiphop's substance.

The lowlife tall tales on *Doggystyle* are lively, vivid examples of Black folks acting wild. Dr. Dre ignores how Black folks express themselves in favor of how they destroy themselves. As comical and rhythmic as Dr. Dre can make these horror stories—and as cleverly as Snoop can narrate them—the more they allow for escapist displacement of genuine rage. There's nothing on *Doggystyle* that isn't a disgrace to hiphop as a politicized pop form made by alert, thinking young artists—part of a generation that had inherited some real benefits from the sixties struggle. And this is what must have turned Tupac's jailhouse envy into desperation. This regressive rap is for the budded and the stunted—a world of topsyturvy ethics that paralleled Tupac's jail-cell hell.

Some observers have termed this funkified West Coast illin' as nihilistic. It's actually much simpler than that: the wit in Snoop's vocal inflections displays a method of speaking/performing that is fully conscious of the pleasures in dialect and slang. He raps carefully, for the love of speech, and for sheer conviviality. Like Dr. Dre, with his tried-and-true appropriations of the oldest, most familiar P-Funk riffs, Snoop follows the most commercial aspects of hiphop performance. In doing this, rappers may lose touch with the music's protesting value, but they are not nihilistic; they're proudly capitalistic. In contemplating the *Doggystyle* sales phenomenon, *The New York Times* also hopped on the bandwagon, promoting the album even before hearing it. Tupac's line—*"a lot like a crap game"*—expresses a vague awareness of the convergence of hiphop ambition and corporate instinct—two streams merging in a river of greed

When Tupac, with Rev. Daughtry's approval, chose "Temptations" as his next release, his unconscious intent was to highlight the slack, stereotyped image which had made Snoop and Dr. Dre the first Black rap stars to grace the cover of *Rolling Stone*. That image may also go some way to explain why MTV has devoted so much airtime to Death Row videos and to its rappers' courtroom shenanigans. *Doggystyle* makes humor out of the Black deprivation , disguising it as fun. On "Gz and Hustlas," Snoop creates a schoolroom fantasy where he aspires to be a hustler, suggesting that the smart kid chooses crime and gets over. It was a stale routine when Ice Cube tried something like it back on *Amerikka's Most Wanted* in 1990, but it epitomizes the glorification of a ghetto myth. Just as Dr. Dre's music videos instituted a film genre made up of hitting switches, drinking 40s, and dancehall grooving that is now imitated by most rap artists seeking a similar crossover success, "Gz and Hustlas" distills a version of Black experience that can easily be sold and digested without changing the life or thinking of anyone—Black or White—who hears it. Tupac, newly released from jail, stepped into this void. And though a posthumous *Spin* magazine reference asserts that Tupac "polarized the races like few pop stars, in death as in life," this hot new hiphop style offers only an apathetic response to the new realities of social and racial collapse.

Doggystyle's deliberately-fashioned West Coast street-life sounds suggest a potential numbness in the mindless beats. Twenty-year old George Clinton's funk riffs, unconnnected to a modern sense of agitation, stop being melodic, stop dead in the groove—emotionally static. The best hiphop encourages listeners to *move*; but this stuff anesthetizes, pacifies, allows the infiltration of destructive, selfish motives. The romantic descriptions of brutality that Dre and Snoop (and later Tupac) purvey shatter all notions of good will and racial unity. This is, actually, anti-funk: It traduces Clinton's spaced-out, feel-good-but-still-political fantasies.

It is not adventurous music. For proof, recall the amazing, booming cellos on Public Enemy's "Anti-Nigger Machine" (a tune and title worthy of Mingus). The 1990 track not only pushed pop music structures forward but also advanced the possibility of rejecting slackness. Rejecting the romance of the gun, Chuck D says: *"I never had to be bad/My mama raised me mad"*—a line Tupac should have remembered in that it opposes hardness with intelligence—"mad" being a state of mental preparedness. And behind it all, in that buttery way Public Enemy's cello sound expands the vibe, it links its political message to ineffable sensual pleasure, to love.

The only sign of affection on *Doggystyle* is Snoop's "Lodi Dodi," a tribute/cover of Slick Rick's "La Dee Da Di." Snoop hooks into Slick Rick's fear and loathing and comical vanity, but he doesn't reveal much of himself, although self-exposure is part of what made "La Dee Da Di" remarkable. Snoop has bit-ten Slick Rick's vocal elasticity but he can't dope out his genius, so this version has only shock value, not horror. Slick Rick's confession about all kinds of sex-ual entrapment seems merely misogynist when Snoop raps it, whereas the mean-ness Slick Rick showed to women—with his vocal tricks, veering from testos-terone roughness to estrogen squeaks, and feigned confidence—opened up a whole world of male insecurity and urban instability to public view.

Black male insecurities are a rash that spreads mangelike throughout *Doggystyle*, even when stylishly rendered by individualistic Dogg Pound rap-pers. Snoop plays with this insanity on "Murder Was the Case," a poor imita-tion of Geto Boys' tragic rap theater that knowingly flirts with Snoop's real-life situation as a murder suspect. The remorselessness is rote, but the shameless self-exploitation (something Tupac would soon emulate) is horrendous. Who is this song for? Without confronting fear, it lies to the boys in the 'hood even as it beguiles a crossover audience who may enjoy it—and the next track, "Serial Killa"—as cartoons. Significantly, the cover art of the *Doggystyle* album *is* a car-toon—a crude imitation of Pedro Bell's ingeniously complex funkadelic album graphics. Snoop and Dr. Dre obviously have no delusions; they present them-selves as cartoons and as fuck-ups to please a paying audience.

When seventies soul group The Dramatics (yes, The Dramatics) are enlist-ed to provide background harmonies on "Doggy Dogg World," it is an uncon-vincing attempt at legitimatizing gangsta stress. Problem is: *Doggystyle* is a long way from the devastating/ecstatic precision and profundity of the blues. The Dramatics come off sounding just as venal as Tha Dogg Pound—Jimmy Iovine, Dr. Dre, and Calvin Broadus, who identifies himself most often not as a Black man but as a dog.

These aren't the predomi-nant sounds folks live by but it's the way a racist social system encourages them to live—and die.

WHY AM I SO BLIND?
WHY AM I SO HIGH?
I DON'T KNOW

goes an exchange on "Gz Up, Hoes Down." It's a cry for help, of course, but no answer or help will come from an audience entertained by Snoop's self-immolation, whether they be white slummers or Blacks in the slammer like Tupac.

NOTORIOUS **B.I.G.**

Everett Collection

While Snoop was being celebrated by the mainstream, the best hardcore solo rapper of the era was, in fact, The Notorious B.I.G., who displayed the most advanced rapping skills since Slick Rick. Tupac had befriended B.I.G. in New York, then they fell out over the usual boy-boy squabbles: "My rap is stronger than yours!" "I don't care," Tupac is remembered saying, "Biggie slams!" Yet personal animosity escalated to professional rivalry, Tupac even used the 1996 MTV Awards Show to taunt Biggie with ugly boasts about sexing his wife, singer Faith Evans, as well as blaming Biggie and Bad Boy Entertainment President Sean "Puffy" Combs for the 1994 shooting incident which almost cost Tupac his life. Now, it hurt to be in jail watching his rivals living larger.

With the release of his debut album, *Ready to Die*,

Biggie's bruiser image made him hiphop's equivalent to a Hollywood block-buster. "Gimmie the Loot" is an extravaganza that is funnier, scarier, more complicated and more interesting than *Menace II Society, Boyz N the Hood, Straight Out of Brooklyn, Fresh* and most hiphop records put together. No wonder he and Tupac first got along; the rapper on his way to being a movie star surely related to the Brooklyn rapper who was already a star in his heart.

"Gimmie the Loot" jumps. You understand instantly why the album is so popular. Chris Wallace, a rotund young man of twenty-four recording as The Notorious B.I.G., was as big as life. Answering to Biggie Smalls (the nickname teases size with intricacy), he looked like the kind of kid who had developed humor and cool as a defense against ridicule. And because he stayed alert to the rude, funny ways people speak and behave, you feel alive listening to him. But since Biggie doesn't go any further than that, his album *Ready to Die* is also enomously problematic.

Playing a subway-robber as brash, recognizable and hyped-up as James Cagney , Biggie and his partner trade verses in a hell-raising spree. (A tease, *"I'm a bad, bad boy,"* echoes in the background.) Biggie busts the vehemence of young Black criminals who mix up a heritage of oppression and poverty then act out a mean, moral rebellion. *"You ain't gots to explain shit! I been robbin' muthafuckas since the slave ship!"* This must be the single most outrageous rap line since Slick Rick's "La Dee Da Di" and it's so ignorant it resonates. "Gimme the Loot," like a thirties gangster movie (or DePalma's 1983 updated *Scarface*) is in the spirit of retribution and impudence: the most desperate youth indulge in wickedness (a term consonant with Biggie's West Indian ancestry) to prove that they are, after all, human. Biggie and his boy prey on their own people cuz who else will care? Their social perversion is delineated in a rhyme partially borrowed from Tupac's *Strictly for my N.I.G.G.A.Z.*:

```
            Big up! Big up!
        It's a stick up, stick up
I'm shootin' niggas quicker if you hiccup
```

"Gimme the Loot" trades Public Enemy's cultural solidarity for filthy lucre—it portrays a genuine, lower-depths depravity. Seeing a well-dressed sister, Biggie's stick-up pal squeals, *"Oooh Biggie, let me jack her! I kick her in the back! Hit her with the gat!"* And Biggie answers, *"Chill Shorty, let me do that."*

This horribly funny track makes a boast out of the worst things Black folks can do to each other. Its vicious descriptions of envy and calibrated aggression are also intimately recognizable, easily mistaken for glamour yet dramatizing society's actual "no hope" desperation which Biggie isn't about to deny. This dread truth, turned jolly and big as life, makes "Gimmie the Loot" an unconscious satire on need-turned-to-greed. Its shootout ending isn't tough enough on the ghetto fantasy of power, but it's closer to being the comic-tragic masterpiece that *The Chronic* meant to be.

There's a clever spin on every cut of *Ready to Die*, illuminating the subjects beyond one-dimensional boasting or simple exposition. The sex track "One More Chance," so full of pungent descriptions, is underscored by "%!*@ Me (Interlude)," which makes good on Biggie's proclaimed "stroke of genius" with a hump-and-response dialogue structure. It's a parody of sex talk as well as a satire of Black stereotypes:

**GANGSTA KILLIN',
CHRONIC SMOKIN',
OREO COOKIE EATIN',
PICKLE JUICE DRINKIN',**

The humor complicates the track, combining pornography with ethnography and, making a good-natured crack at his own physiognomy, becoming art at the end when Biggie, busting his nut and a bed spring, says to his girl, *"I'm sorry."* Flipping "One More Chance's" cunnilingus-as-a-sign-of-prowess, he mocks his own male selfishness and clumsiness.

But "%!*@ Me (Interlude)" is absolutely *not* clumsy. There's intelligence and sophistication in Biggie's self-deprecating honesty. Here, typical hiphop tropes are used—endorsed—but also tested by absolute charm, artistry, and wit.

"Warning clicks with the right invective, the appropriate, dirty dare (Biggie's "I get hard core" is way more fly than the "get medical" in *Pulp Fiction*.) The fun is mistaken for a justified response to dangerous circumstances as with Dr.Dre, Snoop and stupid-acting rappers. This may be fun, it may be macho, but it's also childish.

Call it perspective. That's what separates *Ready to Die* from most other hiphop albums. Biggie's opportunity for living phat could have just caused him to rehash the ghetto stereotypes of *Straight Out of Brooklyn* or even of the unmanageable Wu-Tang Clan—but there's a richer sensibility here. Biggie's perspective isn't forthright or transcendent like Public Enemy's, De La Soul's or Arrested Development's—it's worldly. Like the best solo rap artists—L.L. Cool J., Scarface, Slick Rick, Ice Cube, and sometimes Tupac—Biggie pulls his own weight and views his own course. I don't think his stubborn social sense, his engagement with low-living, is necessarily a truer artistry (he's a serious Biz Markie), but it represents the basic decency of an individual *thinking out* a suppressed culture's isolated politics.

Ready to Die shows Biggie to be fully responsive to the world, but the closest Biggie gets to understanding the world is to reason *"I rob and steal cuz money got that whip appeal."* The personal disclosure in those lines is recognizable to every rapper and rap fan; you pick up the gist of those lines in every instance of Biggie's and Tupac's bluster: The hurt fuels the yearning; the burning desire obscures a more political focus on how either Biggie or Tupac can achieve what he really needs. Perhaps it was because they shared both this longing and this incapacity that they eventually broke ranks—it certainly accounts for their flamboyant presence in hiphop.

The way Puffy Combs' love of voices and Easy Mo Bee's tactile production works, *Ready to Die* reaches out to pinch you. And the pinch feels like a tickle, especially when Biggie blows himself away and the album ends with aural evidence of life going on (the phone company's mechanical message, a friend's exasperated hang-up). These sounds echo callousness and helplessness, but they never quite erase the voice of Biggie's very human, very hiphop dejection: This, too, is art.

The album's title, *Ready to Die*, suggests the handy, marketable nihilism that makes Nas' debut album, *Illmatic*, seem accomplished but suspect (largely fake, corporate rap). Biggie, in the way of street storytellers and neophyte ghetto griots, means something more interesting than literally being ready to die. The obverse of these words is the subtext of the entire album—at this moment, Biggie is *alive*.

Little Kim, Notorious B.I.G., and Sean "Puffy" Combs at the 1995 Billboard Music Awards.

Biggie's extravagance—like Tupac's feistiness—was something that fans could relate to without the need for a publicity machine. There's a common quality of humor and earnestness related to an ardent involvement with the ideas and language of a culture that makes a rapper big—a genuine folk star—even outside the mainstream's purview.

With success, Tupac tried to maintain a generous sympathy with the 'hood life he came from. Following Melle Mel's Old School rap *"I'm a bow-legged brother . . . there'll never be another/ I bought a mansion for my mother,"* Tupac would live with his mother in a newly purchased San Fernando Valley home that one journalist described as "a pretty blue-and-white house on a quiet tree-lined street." But that change in lifestyle actually changed little that really mattered; as much as he craved it, it wasn't always easy for Tupac to contend with fame and success. On the *Poetic Justice* Bay Area set, homies insisted he acknowledge them during a shot. When a journalist pointed out their presence, Tupac answered:

The young bucks are gonna be jealous. Some older people, too. They got mad because I used to be their gofer. They used to run me to the store. They're sitting there knowing they used to give me money to go to the store. They're sitting there knowing they used to give me money to go to the store and now I've got their whole family taking pictures with me. That's an animosity that nothing I can do can kill, because that's poverty shit and I can understand.

Given Tupac's empathy, it's surprising his jail experience didn't produce a song that takes humorous account of that all-American misadventure. But Tupac wasn't interested in that kind of contemplation. He wanted to be back on top of the rap game, reveling in hiphop's ribald view of the world. Instead, it was comic rapper Coolio (Artis Ivey) who came up with the classic, "Mama, I'm in Love Wit a Gangsta"—a song that opens the rap convict's heart, divulging insecurities Tupac could not articulate.

This song, a duet with female sex rapper LeShaun, conveys the ghetto ethos the way people live it. Like YoYo's "Letter to the Pen," the impassioned feminine perspective uncovers a surprisingly poignant side. The reality of lockdown isn't just about the imprisonment of lovers, parents, or children but about the breakdown of social ambitions and cultural expectations.

LeShaun's drowning-in-the-sea-of-love confession can be heard as a sociological report—the news is in her voice: helpless, proud, excited, and *unsure*, LeShaun conveys the complex emotions of a girl who's gone past innocence. Think of all the genre movies where women fell for gunslingers and bootleggers yet kept their honor. They could have divulged some of Leshaun's ambivalence, but the old forms didn't allow these women to be openly conscious of their feelings. Brazen LeShaun and clear-eyed Coolio match wits to make a hiphop *Sense and Sensibility*. Truer to Jane Austen than to Madonna's "Material Girl" or Whitney Houston's "The Greatest Love of All," "Mama, I'm in Love Wit a Gangsta" concentrates on an individual's social engagement, her self-surprising ability to love.

Coolio is so plugged in his braids stand up as if electrified. He's sensitive to the *people*, both those who sadly get taken and those desperate to have fun. In his rap sketches someone always pays for ghetto transactions. Coolio gets serious without sarcasm and so the conventional morality dulls the fact of transgression that L.L. made sting. Yet Coolio's ingenuity shows best in "Mama's" love lyric irony.

Face it: this woman's song, expressing brother- and ghetto-love, is something many male rappers wouldn't dare. Coolio and LeShaun represent ruffneck magnetism as an ambisexual thing. The setup is a young woman's response to her man spending jail time, going beyond the surface concerns (as seen in Darnell Martin's movie *I Like It like Tha*t). LeShaun makes sense of her life by describing it:

> Mama (Mama) I'm in love wit a gangsta
> And I know he's a killer
> But I love dat nigga

The echoed "Mama" is the sound of conscience; LeShaun balks at old morality, yet hesitates like a child before a parent. That's the song's dramatic tension—both Coolio, raging on the phone from the pen, and LeShaun, trying to raise her kids and stay true to their daddy, are straining to fit their emotions into a rough reality. LeShaun's *"I love dat nigga"* is, in fact, pathetic: love *plus* resignation.

In this love song, affection conveys shock: the truth is—even in debased circumstances people live, people love. There's no pretense; the killer she loves isn't honorable, just a man of his time. "Mama, I'm in Love Wit a Gangsta" is straight up about the guilt and hard work of modern love in which everybody knows/loves somebody who isn't innocent.

This song brings us back to the dilemma Tupac faced in jail watching, listening, and coveting the new gangsta rap success from inside the house of pain. Revealing young Black men's vulnerability—and the devotion of their people on the outside—it's a song that typifies fans' feelings for Tupac. It's got to be more than the face and it isn't merely the voice. It's what he stands for as the misunderstood Black male who warms the hearts of those who also feel cheated, mistreated, or simply unappreciated.

If loving Tupac is wrong, his fans reject the propriety of judging men by the standards of an unjust society. They love him for what they recognize as the sincere, pure part of themselves and the other fallible/lovable men in their lives. Snoop has only a bit of this; Dr. Dre and terror-bear "Suge" Knight have none; but you can bet they recognized it in Tupac's matinee idol impact.

After he'd been released from jail and signed with Death Row, a reporter observed Shakur fronting for Knight at a Los Angeles food benefit:

It was Thanksgiving and the gangstas were giving out turkeys in the ghetto. A line snaked down the steps round the side, and along the block of a South Central Los Angeles community center. The free food paid for by Death Row, was supposed to be doled out at 11 in the morning. The annual event gave Knight a chance to show off Shakur as his latest signing. . . but the pair had yet to show. So the old folks and the moms with babies in their arms waited patiently, staring through the windows at the stacks of frozen turkeys locked

inside. . . A couple of hours later the Death Row car arrived. . . having soothed the hungry, Shakur disappeared into the shadow. He might have been the star, but Knight controlled the vibe and Shakur did nothing to undermine it.

That event has chilling echoes of the disastrous early seventies food giveaway that the Symbionese Liberation Army arranged with the Patty Hearst kidnapping—a grotesque iconographic stunt based on a lordly potentate bidding that his underlings make him look good. Only here Tupac remains the icon, despite whatever actual manipulations of power took place. Tupac's welcome into Death Row, the security he felt in hiphop stardom, was a Symbiotic Liberation for Black protest's dysfunctional scion. Even when he was late or bad, his fans felt good vibes. That Thanksgiving reporter also noted "Everyone was unbearably polite. 'Free Tupac!' people began chanting. Only slowly did another chant replace it: 'Fuck Tupac! Free the turkeys!'"

Such emotional range requires genuine affection. The artist formerly known as MC New York had achieved his own "Fuck with 'Pac Day."

CHAPTER 15
the charts: shake it, baby!

the year tupac would not live out

began with MTV Superstardom. On January 1, 1996, the music video for *California Love* had its world premiere on MTV—in heavy rotation—serving Tupac to the world on a satellite platter. But *California Love* isn't just a signal of superstardom, it's hiphop's ultimate expression of ambition and indulgence deluxe.

Tupac felt extravagant after Suge Knight visited him in prison with a hand-written contract to join the stable of artists at Death Row Records. "I know business," Knight said. "I know how to take my artists and make them super-star status, and make them get what they deserve." In collaboration with Dr. Dre, Knight had founded an empire based on a new hiphop phase and a dis-tinctive sound that put California hiphop on the map; it was stronger than any-

Death Row Records co-founder Marion "Suge" Knight and his attorney, Richard Hirsch, appear in the Criminal Courts Building in Los Angeles, Monday Oct. 28, 1996, and is charged with violating his probation.

AP/Wide World Photos

thing from the Bay Area. Tupac was already impressed by it and signed the contract in haste. Knight put up over $1 million in bail, freeing Tupac from institutional bondage and committing him to three albums for Death Row records.

"I don't think he had a choice," Afeni said of the transaction. "And I'm sure he didn't feel like he had a choice under the circum-stances." No one else was posting bond and Tupac had been ready for freedom a long time—since before birth, Afeni says. Tupac responded to his new boss as if to the big brother he had never had—with gratitude and blind trust. Afeni remembers, "He got out of prison on Thursday and by Thursday night he was in California in the studio. By Friday he had completed seven songs from that double album."

Afeni's skeptical view has a special significance in light of her own release to give birth to her son 24 years earlier. Very different circumstances had deliv-ered Tupac from jail to indentured service. And he seemed to respond to his release with a naive enthusiasm that had no room for suspicion. Though able to turn slick phrases, he didn't see the irony in leaving lockdown for Death Row—a company whose name and commitment suggested no way out.

Fresh out of the slammer, he could scoff at the social system that had punished him by embracing the insolence implicit in the name Death Row—a name that put the spotlight on Black doom, and particularly the Dread fate of the 25 percent of Black American youths who languish behind bars in some house of pain.

"When you sign to Death Row you sign for life," was a cautionary pun among hiphop journalists. Rumors suggested that Tupac had been "bought" for a million dollars; that his artistic freedom would amount to a sharecropper's existence— like Snoop Doggy Dogg's indebtedness that kept him at Death Row even after Dr. Dre had severed ties with Knight.

Afeni set a high value on

Tupac Shakur and Snoop Doggy Dogg at the 1996 MTV Video Music Awards

Andrea Renault/Globe Photos

freedom. She knew, "Once someone buys you, they own you." What she couldn't understand was how Tupac could fall for just the kind of enticement he had always ragged on.

Go back to "Young Niggaz" on *Me Against the World*—written and recorded before Tupac's desperation—to find his warning to *"young niggas in a rush to be gangstas."* His advice: *"Muthafuckaz need to just calm down/ And peep what the fuck they want to do with the rest of they life/ Before you end your life before you begin your life."* His own words should have cautioned him

"Muthafuckaz need to just calm down

And peep what the fuck they want to do with the rest of they life

Before you end your life before you begin your life."

against his rush to join Death Row. Instead, Tupac saw only the quantum leap his career would take. Being accepted by the Southern California branch of hiphop meant more than a merger; it promised acceptance in a fraternity. Following all the tension and trouble in New York—the shooting, the rivalry with Biggie, the jail time—Tupac's sense of betrayal was brightened by Knight, who had indeed stepped in like a rescuing knight to offer the rapper a second, bigger chance at stardom.

All Eyez on Me is widely referred to as rap's first double album—a distinction that rightfully belongs to DJ Jazzy Jeff and the Fresh Prince's *I'm the DJ, He's the Rapper*. But Tupac's fourth album was actually rap's first double CD, a major push toward recognition. Sex is the sound of "California Love," Tupac's first Number One single. It certifies a level of achievement, of rap triumph, and American commercial bliss. It's also the expression/emission of Roger Troutman. And Dr. Dre, who produced "California Love," gets props for reviving Troutman's "sound" and fitting it to Tupac's ecstasy. As the lead exponent of the eighties dance group Zapp ("Computer Love" was it's big 1986 hit), Troutman innovated a rhythmic vocal distortion that wove through the band's basic funk grooves. His eerily sensual vocal contrasts could be hard to take, yet it's one of those signature sounds of individual genius that occur throughout the history of Black pop. (On Scritti Politti's 1989 *Provision*, Green Gartside enlisted Troutman, along with Miles Davis, to augment his exquisitely high-tech pop deconstruction on the tracks of "Boom! There She Was, " and especially "Sugar and Spice,"where Troutman sang the extremes of nearly inexpressible physical release.)

Troutman's high squeak and low-pitch warbles turn up on "California Love" to sexualize Dre's particular politics, where prosperity equals orgasm. No one expected a love song from the cold-hearted maestro of gangsta rap but "California Love" commemorates Tupac's flight west after his East Coast jail bail-out. The song celebrates the social haven (gold mine) Dre and Suge Knight invite Tupac to join. It's not the sunny California of teenage fun that The Beach Boys created, but something darker, more evanescent, and mercenary. Dre mystifies success as "love," then raps about California as the locale of his professional and cultural "triumph."

There's a mythological—and historical—background to that victory: West Coast hiphop is that area's strongest Black musical achievement. It's an empire of sorts—and success within the genre is a dream to a generation of Black working class kids whose parents suffered through that Republican community's severe racial redistricting—even after numbers of them had fled to California from far worse conditions in the American South. For many, the dream of hiphop success is still deferred. Yet the electricity of a record like "California Love" shocks the ghost of Tom Joad, just as it mocks the real-life efforts of Cesar Chavez and denies the life of George Jackson.

Like Brian Wilson, Dre had tapped into a primal American dream, albeit of a less innocent era. "F——Wit Dre Day" (1993) first claimed this mythological territory when Dre rapped *"Is it Dre?/ That's what they say everyday in L.A."* and since then, he'd only blown-up bigger. Dre's heinous rap topics (favoring Black self-destruction, class animosity, and racial stereotype) his gin-and-juice-soaked vision still fakes Black solidarity by putting forth his own good time to others. Those euphoric beats in "California Love" aren't an escape from O.J. Simpson's L.A. but a denial of contemporary stress. And for four minutes, as Dre, Roger, and Tupac salute brothers up and down the California Coast— San Diego, Long Beach, Compton, Watts, San Francisco, Oakland—it's almost convincing. In "California Love," Dre creates a sense of belonging that neglects rap protest, preferring an affirmation that is vaguely patriotic. He doesn't groove to real life struggle but to successful capitalist competition—his own genius triumphant. Tupac grooved to it big time.

It's a millionaire's view, happily ignorant of California's Black history (as partly told in Mike Davis' *City of Quartz*) where only a celebrity like Nat King Cole could break the housing color bar. Roger Troutman's role in Dre's victory song shows an ironic, partial alliance—but don't be misled, it's just show business. In 1986, at Zapp's peak, a *Jet* magazine article detailed how Roger and his bandmate-brothers Lester, Larry, and Zapp joined with their other siblings, Rufus, Janet and Loretta to build more than 100 low-cost houses in their hometown, Dayton, Ohio. (Accomplished with loans from Warner Bros. and Lefrak Entertainment Company, this is the kind of genuine political action overlooked by the *New York Times* when they tout Suge Knight and his shifting fortunes with Interscope Records.)

Roger told *Jet*:

The Black community is indeed our responsibility. You're obligated to people if they support you, you're obligated to your roots, no matter what they are. Everyone loves where they come from and if you're not proud of where that is, you should go back and do something about it.

Dre himself never tries to sound like a politician when party throwing will do. "California Love" lowers the bass on the same ear-stunning tintinnabulation that made a hit of 1995's "Keep Their Heads Ringin,'" but turns up the sonic whip. "Inglewood's always up to no good," he says, ambiguously. For both of them, America—California—is a party 'cause it's where they can fulfill their love of money. And Tupac has accepted the invitation.

"California Love" has a quasi-Republican ethos in the way it substitutes feel-good sentiment and sensation for social action. It launched the release of Tupac's two-CD album *All Eyez on Me* with Tupac playing the hyped-up Black ne'er-do-well to perfection. A dull rapper compared to Dre, who masters a functional snarl, Tupac has little to do with this record's beauty—he's still a student to his producer's savvy in the fame game. Dre has the best lines, carried by sheer audacity and rhyme, updating California's sun-fun myth as a defense against depression: "Like a vest for your jimmy in the city of sex."

> On a mission for them greens
> Lean, mean, money-makin' machine servin' fiends
> I been in the game for ten years makin' rap tunes
> Ever since honeys was wearin' Sassoons
> Now its 95 and they clock me and watch me
> Diamond-shinin', lookin' like I robbed Liberace
> It's all good from Diego to the Bay
> Your city is the bomb if your city's makin' pay.

Tupac's sex-grunt "Umpf!" can be heard in the background. Troutman's sizzling counterpoints (*"Come on, come on;" "California knows how to party"*) epitomize how Dre and Tupac get off on the commercialization of Black lawlessness through the sensual distraction of artistic recreation.

Dre gets thrilling effects from mixing fancy JB-horn toots and rumbling piano rhythms with Troutman's orgasmic stutters. It's a live and large production, revving up the old notion that gangstas and criminals are sexy into a more precise frenzy. The freedom implicit in their anti-social acts gives them allure. "California Love" uses Roger's artistic simulation of sexual thrill to proclaim the power Dre must feel every day in L.A., knowing his effects on the dreams of hiphop's fans and enemies. It's devastating when Roger follows Dre's rap with a one-man chorus that doubly puns:

SHAKE, SHAKE iT, BABY
SHAKE, SHAKE iT, MAMA
SHAKE, SHAKE iT, CALi

Hiphop has certainly rocked the authoritarian world of C. Delores Tucker and Bill Bennett; its success can indeed seem earthshaking to musicians benefitting from its quasi-revolution. After the seventies British group The Clash had done its job, frontman Joe Strummer tried to keep going and put out an eighties album titled *Earthquake Weather*, a lame effort, still holding on to the idea of creating pop art that can change things aesthetically and for real. It happens that Black-American artists who triumph over daily social oppression can automatically achieve the subversive effect white artists construct through theory and illusion. Both Dre and Troutman—even Tupac—understood that hiphop's cultural influence had shaken America where it lives and dreams. Movement and money define the country. But the song didn't become a hit until the pop mix was re-released in the summer of '96." At that point, "California Love" finally caught on as the stress of the year amped and the rappers' release could really be felt. "The track hits your eardrums like a slug to your chest, " Dre raps as the music changes the listener's metabolism, offering instant escape and elevation. It's elemental, similar to the texture-based smash success of Coolio's "Gangsta's Paradise."

These records signify a huge change in pop evolution, certainly an increase in thematic harshness since Stevie Wonder's "Pasttime Paradise." Now, gorgeous string arrangements—unheard for two decades—struck the modern hiphop audience as an unexpected epiphany, giving elegance and elevation to Coolio's litany of ghetto strife. These kids had no idea that Wonder's original song had spoken out against mid-seventies apathy by creating nostalgia for a still earlier, better time. Hiphop audiences brought their own political concerns—looking beyond apathy into a hopeful hopelessness. This knowledge is central to making sense of the two-hour playing time of *All Eyez on Me*; it's proof of the energy of Black resignation.

All Eyez on Me is made to get blunted to; laying back is a requirement for listening to it. Tupac, here, investigates gangsta rap's scary understanding of Black youth's worst instincts. At first this isn't so easy to discern, but Dre's use of P-Funk beats is a sign of his own indifference. Emulating James Brown riffs would require more smarts, some confrontation with Southern R&B basics rather than George Clinton's protective urban sass. Dre has stated his preference for working with new artists whose voices he can help discover and shape into

self-confidence. And although Dre got it up for the stellar "California Love," he left Tupac on his own to search for a style.

In Mel Watkins' classic study "The Lyrics of James Brown" (1971), he describes the search that happens within Black pop artistry: "One's import does not rest with abstract, societally defined positions or postures, Instead it is situation oriented, constantly reassessed, dependent upon the outcome of each personal confrontation and interaction." In this sense *All Eyez on Me* is a collection of Tupac postures, a one-man filmography of situations, meet-cutes, shoot-outs, money-shots and glamour poses. They may lack Dre's dynamism, but each track is a steady, painstaking display of personal cultural options.

Divided into Books 1 and 2, *All Eyez on Me* parallels Michael Jackson's awesome, intimidating *HIStory*. With *All*

Al Pereira/Michael Ochs Archives

Eyez on Me, Tupac, in the 'nineties, as much as James Brown in the 'seventies, affirms his shared acceptance of life's absurdities and jiving. But a close listen to this good-time album reveals a contradiction to Watkins' thesis. In honoring James Brown as a bedrock modern artist, Watkins was speaking of his effect on a more cohesive, saner Black community. Tupac records for a changed, debased community that regales crime and violence as a "mythic deviation."

If *All Eyes on Me* is not gangsta rap's best album, it holds its position as the form's magnum opus. Every track plays out the gangsta mythology that sustains today's desolate young Black community. It's key subjects are sexual pleasure and male competition, but where James Brown once embodied these themes (Watkins credits Brown's performance as "authentic" and his lyrics with "meaning that transcends mere sexuality [with] social meaning [that is] readily understood by Black audiences") Tupac merely mimes them. Only a few of these tracks are so deeply imagined that one can say Tupac embodies their subject. His contradictory compassion and disdain from song to song makes the album a chain of oddly-cut links:

book one:

Ambitionz As a Ridah—"*I'm on a meal ticket mission*" Tupac begins, observing ghetto chaos: "*Niggas is jealous/ Deep inside they wanna be me.*" "*It was my ambition to rise above these jealous motherfuckers.*" To dramatize the disorder, producer Dat Nigga Daz keeps Tupac's voice level with the bass mix. Chaos and competition.

All Bout U—"*Every other city we go, every other video no matter where we go I see the same ho's*" goes the chorus made up of Tupac, Snoop Doggy Dogg, and Nate Dog. "*I'm a thug nigga, I love niggas,*" plies the fantasy of hiphop rollin'. It's more ambitious but never sanctimonious: Snoop mentions seeing the same "bitch" in Warren G and Tupac videos, also seen at the Million Man March. Lyrically, the put-down crosses gender as in Apache's "Gangsta Bitch." It's ambivalence puts "You're So Vain" in the context of ghetto jealousy.

Skandalouz—Turned on by skeezers, Tupac puts them down. Shame rears it's head. Look out: He's scandalized.

Got My Mind Made Up—*"Get off my coat/ Clearin' my throat"*—a blues reference via The Beastie Boys. The past is alive: *"Smilin' faces deceive,"* Redman says in a conversation with Tupac, Dat Nigga Daz, Kurupt, and Method Man. An echoing drum beat measures their reinforced distrust. Each bro builds up the other's paranoia.

How Do U Want It—*"Comin' up as a nigga in a cash game/ Living in the fast lane"*—a sequel to Jodeci's *The Concert, The Afterparty, the Hotel,* a landmark of the pimpology that infects hiphop. Jodeci's K.C. sings the sexual metaphor of what is really a fuck-off to Tupac's critics. The rhyme *"Delores Tucker you a motherfucker instead of tryin' to help a nigga you destroy a brother,"* begins a list of sucker politicians. It makes subversive use of Quincy Jones' "Body Heat;" producer Johnny J finds it a classical expression of Black achievement.

2 of Amerikaz Most Wanted—*"Nothing but a gangsta party,"* Snoop agrees with Tupac. Happy to stroll along Death Row, they dive into the stereotypes that previously chafed them.

No More Pain—*"When I die I want to be a living legend."* Alize and Cristal set the mood for a martyr's consumption and belligerence. *"They shot me five times but real niggass don't die/ Death is reincarnation/ I came to bring the pain hardcore to the brain."* Funereal elegance borrowed from Jodeci producer DeVante Swing. There's a correlation between the slick life of amoral sensuality and immoral revenge, *"Retaliation is a must."* Death is the only relief Tupac offers, cheering "Thug Life!" at the end.

Heartz of Men—Tupac tells Suge Knight to watch him get even. *"I'm gonna start diggin' to these nigga's chest. Friends vs. Enemies."* And *"It's a dirty game/ Y'all gotta be careful who you fuck with."* He doubles the meaning of "fuck with" but the complication is spoken more to himself. Reference to Mr. Makaveli introduces his vengeful alter-ego. Richard Pryor's "That Nigger's Crazy" sample makes comic-drama of fearful retaliation

Life Goes On—In a mellower mood, a reminiscence song. *"How many brothers fell victim to the street/ Rest in peace young nigga there's a heaven for a G."* Well set up with a grungy detail, *"I got your name tatted on my arm, so we both bond til the day I die."* A key song, if only for the way sentiment interrupts the troublesome parlaying of responsibility to "the street." Still, the musical sway can carry a listener to maudlin softness. It recalls the way Ice Cube's "Dead Homiez" pioneered this sense of loss.

Only God Can Judge Me—*"In my mind, I'm a blind man doin' time"* *"They say it's the white man I should fear, but it's my own kind doin' all the killin' here."* Zig-zag beats cushion Tupac's simple delivery; the points touch neatly. *"And all my memories is seein' brothers bleed"* or *"I'm havin' nightmares, homicidal fantasies."* Movin' from Geto Boys to Prince (*'Cuz even doves cry but does God care?"*), Tupac gathers together pop's most accomplished tropes of wonderment. It's an effort to make sense, but there is no intellectual movement here; no investigation. Shallowness comes in blurts.

Tradin' War Stories—*"A military mind/ A criminal grind."* Makaveli comes up again, *"Mama sent me to play with the drug dealers"*—if this is true, it's a shock, full of resentment, presented in a cool, leisurely manner. Dramacyde's soft, feminine background attempts to soothe—like the strings in "Gangsta's Paradise." There's a good sense of drama in Mike Mosley and Rick Rock's production. The self-sentimentalized invocation of "street soldiers" adds to the comradery, but it still distorts the truth of everyday misery. It's the kind of put-on that only works when done in passing conversation, but as an extended metaphor (*"Outlaws on the rise/ Jealous niggas I despise/ Look in my eyes"*) this song focuses on animosity, not on aggrieved sides in an argument. *"It's what players do,"* he tells us. For Tupac, playin' is all.

"California Love (RMX)"—Slowed down from the magnificent pop mix, it fits a buddha buzz. No version of this record is bad; the plus here is Roger Troutman's coda. *"Shake it, Cali"* his computer whines—to his ideal woman? L.L. Cool J.'s? Or maybe even to the earth that moved under Carole King's feet?

I Ain't Mad at Cha—*"Whatever it takes to get you niggas out the 'hood."* That's superficial encouragement, but there's tangible love here, from the words of forgiveness to the blessed Stevie Wonder-style humming in back. Better than "Tradin' War Stories," it puts boyish squabbling in proper proportion. This, at least, is a genuine youth's insight, including his pleas to mama.

What'z Ya Phone #—Riding the groove of The Time's *"777-9311,"* Tupac's comic ribaldry pivots on his sly use of *"fuck with me"* to make phone sex sizzle—a distanced bluff of prowess. It's an inadvertent metaphor for a recording artist's put-on. *"I'm fixin' to come over there,"* he says but as most Tupac fans must attest—he never comes.

book 2:

Can't C Me—In retrospect this song would seem to fuel "Tupac Is Alive!" speculation, but it's really a boast of slipperiness, shamelessly suggesting some craven deliberateness in Tupac's multiple personalities and points of view. No real pleasure in his chameleon self-image is evident, but Dre makes this track funk harder than anything else on the album. A tough joke, if not a good one.

Shorty Wanna Be a Thug—*"Said he wanna be/ One day he gonna be,"* goes this bedtime story. But in narrating a thug life saga, Tupac reveals more about his own ambition than any appeal he might have for youngbloods. Still, Dre's *The Chronic* told this story better in "L'il Ghetto Boy."

Holla at Me—In the person of his left-behind homies, Tupac fears for his own estrangement. *"Gotta be careful/can't let the evil of the money trap me,"* is a class-war principle, not often stated. Although about himself, it can be heard—especially in the jail verse—as Tupac's most empathetic composition.

Wonda Why They Call U Bitch—*"You leave your kids with your mama cuz you headin' for the club,"* Tupac admonishes young mothers. And *"See, I loved you like a sister but you died too quick"* has no compassion. This is moralism, not understanding. Even when he notes *"Dear Miss C. Delores Tucker, you keep stressin' me/ I thought you wanted to know why we call them bitches."* But without realizing any common concern with Miss Tucker, this flipside of "Keep Ya Head Up" shows Tupac can be just as severe and insensitive as his own critics.

When We Ride—"*My name is Makaveli,*" Tupac jokes before flaunting the names of Castro, Khadafi, and Mussolini as troublemaking inspirations. Insipid, but at least DJ Pooh makes the track pump.

Thug Passion—A reworking of Troutman's "Computer Love," so there's some R&B flow. Despite the yen of the female voices—Dramacyde, Jewell and Storm—it's stuck at playing out a boy's fantasy.

Picture Me Rollin'—"*Why niggas look mad? Y'all supposed to be happy.*" Sometimes Tupac's opening lines contain his only complexity. Here he barely sustains the irony in this more serious retake of "Ambitionz of a Ridah." His harried voice sounds *skint* opposite Danny Boy's secure baritone, but the whole thing's about image vs. reality as in the fade-out taunts to the district attorney and police.

Check Out Time—Maybe art imitates life but because the sleaze of on-the-road sex occupies this percolating track, it keeps the husky sounds of guest rappers Kurupt and Big Syke! focussed. Minor, superficial, but smooth.

Ratha Be Ya Nigga—"*I don't want to be yo' man, I want to be ya nigga,*" he trumps The Beatles. "*So I can get drunk and smoke weed all day.*" Tupac attempts to eroticize Black stereotypes that he half believes. His boast, "*A boss player, freaky, motherfucker ghetto dick*" doesn't rise above racism but goes limp before it's restrictions.

All Eyez on Me—"*The fans is watchin'/ Niggas plottin' to get me.*" "*I told the judge I was raised wrong/ And that's why I play shit.*" Not so much a coming clean as self-protective bluster. It's the knowingness of role-playing that makes the beat's monotony wear in—like a threat.

Run Tha Streeetz—Long missing-in-action Michel'le sings support ("*I'll be waiting for you until you get through*"). But the strength of her voice contradicts. Stuck in the background, she sneaks in passionate impatience, giving the lie to so much accumulated fronting.

Aint Hard to Find—*"Waldo?, Waldo?"* says one of the crowd, E-40, B-Legit, C-Bo and Richie Rich. A casual track that affirms we-are-everywhere in Tupac's offhand rhythm. A no-brainer.

Heaven Ain't Hard 2 Find—Feet, balls, and mind on the ground, Tupac rejects pie-in-the-sky for the groove he can get right here and now. The simple, loping beat allows him to deliver his best rap. It's his least sentimental track. Not a song for soldiers but a reach for contentment.

All Eyez on Me's centerpiece CD artwork is a ghetto primitive painting of Tupac and four mates confronting a short-skirted hottie—a reference to the sexual assault that got him in trouble, it creates its own mythology. How can one read this representation of a liquored-up, flirtatious, gang-fronting Tupac, except as the opposite of an idealization—a mean enshrinement of crude living. That puts the graphic in line with the rest of the album. It's a well-programmed, long-winded statement. *"You think we all dogs"* he accuses on the album's closing track but it's part of a complication that Tupac was too enamored of to examine. There's not much more ambition here than simply to impress by size—the album was written and recorded too quickly to have been thought out beyond simple tracks and talented invited guests.

Tupac's intention with *All Eyez on Me* was to rise brazenly from the lower depths of prison with an apotheosis—a deluxe street album. But that's a contradiction in terms, showing either the artist's grandiose silliness or his incapacity. The fact that he could command Death Row's resources to produce a two-disc act of hubris says more about ambition than it does about art—or the understanding of life and humanity that art reveals. Grandstanding, *All Eyez on Me* is impressive, but it speaks less powerfully than simple honesty.

Reborn on two levels, Tupac's rapping in *All Eyez on Me* took on the polyphonic flow that was distinctive to Dre productions; plus, his approach to *"what they say everyday in L.A."* got even wilder. The Death Row principle of artistic behavior, based on movie star/crime star emulation, gave Tupac more opportunity to make theater out of the "revolutionary" urge that seemed no longer possible in the political world of the '90s. Youthful Black activism—essentially a dream of the past—was never more to Tupac than a role to play. He jumped at this moment like an understudy leaping to the lucky break of a stand-in matinee performance. Death Row, an offshoot of Interscope Records (the label founded by producer Jimmy Iovine, an engineer renowned for his pristine work on such seventies rock icons as Bruce Springsteen and Tom Petty), took the idea of corporate independence a step further, prompting a renegade attitude and image that suited Tupac's need for audacity.

Tupac's bleak impudence makes a wry contrast to the dreams of success Dre and Knight sought. It also gave tickling, troubling nuance to the L.A. environment of prosperity and glory that came with the changes Dre instituted to make hiphop an unabashed celebration of power and greed. What's often missed in considerations of Death Row rap is the amount of conscious nihilism being used as an emotional element, if not an operational principle. You could call it jailbird sensibility for its acceptance of demeaning circumstances, fighting degradation with deprecation. That's subtly encoded in the West Coast etymology of "nigger" into "nigga." Death Row rap internalizes Black youth's affront at their social mistreatment with humor. Part of its purposefulness is in ratifying the perhaps necessary psychological trick of finding a way to cope with disparagement, and humor does it fine. The wit of owning "Death Row"—as both a term and label—comes from the reclaimed power of renaming oneself, appropriating government's right to judge and designate. This may be a screwed-up response to authoritarian pressure, but conscious nihilism isn't as pathetic as the unconscious, unrecognized, untraceable sort. Dre clearly understands the socioeconomic conditions he must oppose, and his single-minded success ethic demonstrates a cynicism that shouldn't be confused with nihilism. Death Row records takes a capitalist's approach to nihilism, finding it marketable and relishing the piddling amount of impudence it permits. It fills up that moral hollow where Black pop's heart used to be (you could hear it in such empowering songs of endearment as The Funky Four Plus One's "That's the Joint," De La Soul's "Me, Myself and I" and Son of Bazerk's "One Time For the Rebel").

Death Row's hardened yet affectionate treatment of Black experience matches the complexity of *All Eyez on Me,* where Tupac responds to his own condition, searching for love though deprived of peace. Singing about his own death in "No More Pain" seemed to be the only way he could give clues to feeling enslaved. *"Gotta be careful can't let the evil of the money trap me,"* he said on 'Holler at Me." His convoluted, intertwined affection and aggression cannot be ignored. It remains a part of African-American cultural habit, summoning grace during the effrontery of jesting.

CHAPTER 16 makaveli

tupac learned the Westside sign: closing his thumb in his palm, crossing his middle fingers like a temptress' legs and letting his index finger and pinkie point out to form a proud 'W.' The salute decorates the cover of *All Eyez on Me,* but claiming California as his home wasn't so simple. Tupac found the Southern California style different from both New York and the Bay Area. "I feel like a new kid," an engineer heard him say when he stepped into the studio to record "California Love."

Tupac should have taken heed. Back in the Digital Underground days, Money B had warned Tupac:

> No new niggas. You feel me? 'Cause new niggas always bring problems. You don't know them, you don't know their background. You don't know what they're about. . .

But Tupac was up to his head scarf in new: a new label, a new alter-ego, a new surliness. Through Makaveli, Tupac responded to Death Row's new ruthlessness with a fever. Suge Knight's excitable routines—hard-ass business negotiations, reckless high-rolling—were a source of dismay, even to hyperactive Tupac. Tupac's intimates were mystified to see him take up with this "new nigga" without distancing himself from the combination of Gangsterism and Industry. Incensed by his scraps with Biggie Smalls, resentful of Dr. Dre's defection from Death Row, Tupac's loyalty to Suge Knight only grew. This new nigga, Makaveli, represented a meaner version of going-through-hell hiphop youth, a harsher, even more conflicted Tupac than the Bay Area crew ever could have imagined.

Scott Gordon, an old-school, Oakland-based radio DJ who had known him from the moment he joined the Digital Underground tour, tried to sort out the enigma of Tupac's new surliness:

Suge Knight, he a businessman to all degrees from the street to the major level. To me, 'Pac made a deal with the Devil. 'Pac had everything. He got shot in New York and lived. He talked shit about some of the biggest motherfuckers in New York and he lived. He went to jail, got out on money that Suge Knight gave up. Cars, gold, girls, women, he worked with the biggest artists in the country, movies. He had everything in his hands. And to me, that's something that the Devil gives you. God don't give you all of that. Especially if you sit there and worship money. Money is not what God gives you, it's what the Devil gives you.

Rev. Daughtry also thought Tupac's turmoil came from a spiritual source:

What appeared to us to be his confused, troubled, complex behavior, maybe, maybe, it all stemmed from his fleeing from God. His fighting, his struggling, was at bottom, not so much against society. He was running away from God.

Like Jonah of the Bible, he ran away from God. He created trouble and problems on the ship upon which he tried to escape. The people on the ship decided to throw him to the sea where a big fish was there to swallow him up and once he confessed, agreed to do God's will, the fish spit him up on shore and Jonah did what God wanted. Tupac ran away. He was thrown overboard but there was no big fish to swallow him up and spit him on shore. Or maybe another way of saying it is, when he was swallowed up by the jail system and spit back out on the streets, unlike Jonah, he. . . well. . .

Both of these classic explanations may be behind Tupac telling people, after *All Eyez on Me*, "I'm a living legend." Recognizing his hiphop achievements, he willed status to himself and created a stage name to celebrate it: Makaveli—an ultra-slick reference to the sixteenth century Florentine philosopher Niccolo Machiavelli, best known for political writings which declared power amoral and justified any means to get it. Now Tupac reveled in the double consciousness Rev. Daughtry refers to in religious terms and W.E.B. DuBois wrote about in secular terms, in his 1903 work, *The Souls of Black Folk*:

The Negro is a sort of seventh son, born with a veil, and gifted with second-sight in this American world—a world which yields him no true self-consciousness, but only lets him see himself through the revelation of the other world. It is a peculiar sensation ,this double-consciousness, this sense of always looking at one's self through the eyes of others, of measuring one's soul by the tape of a world that looks on in amused contempt and pity. One every feels his twoness—an American, a Negro; two souls, two thoughts, two unreconciled strivings; two warring ideals in one dark body, whose dogged strength alone keeps it from being torn asunder.

Generations of Black Americans—Panthers and hiphop artists included—have responded in different ways to DuBois' insight, some attempting to prove it wrong or obsolete; but almost all find DuBois' wisdom hard to refute. Even a character as radically conceived as Makaveli fits the description. The artist formerly known as Tupac now *acts* instinctively on the confusions of double-consciousness and the anxieties of modern wickedness, whereas Tupac, originally, had only *reacted* to them.

Bay Area rapper MC Manus, who had moved to Los Angeles since Tupac was in Digital Underground, spoke to Tupac during the recording of *The Don Killuminati The 7-Day Theory*. They had a heart to heart:

> **I could feel his pain. He was committed to life even though he used to say he was 'commuted.' He was set on slanging the bullshit that goes down, but people was tryin' to get him away from the real. I seen this happen to rappers before and told him. He said 'I know Mack, you the king of thieves,' and I said 'Blood, let me tell you your future with Death Row in a minute or less. I'll tell you what comes next. They moguls, man, and the moguls want a human sacrifice. They see a young rapper out here wantin' to make money and they say 'Look at that nigga. He's young, he's hungry—he's perplexed. That's what they say. And they take away the best years of your life. You might think it's all in good fun. But it's up to you to keep your shit clean—get your shit together—if you want to laugh at *them* in the end. If I were you I'd change my name again. They don't care what they do to you, believe me.**

As MC Manus saw Tupac's situation, he had come to feel like a double man. In MC Manus's words "he don't need no mirror to talk to hisself. He was conversatin' in his own head." MC Manus was shocked whenTupac said of Makaveli and the whole hiphop image: "It's up to me to decide when my public image becomes the real thing—whatever the real thing is."

A popular quote among Tupac graveworshippers is "I never had a record *before* I made a record." In a nation where you're unlikely to be arrested if you're rich, that means exactly nothing. As Makaveli, he now intended to justify his bad rep. It's a defensive position—Tupac considered Makaveli a political move, akin to Black impatience and aggravation—and he explained this analogy on MTV:

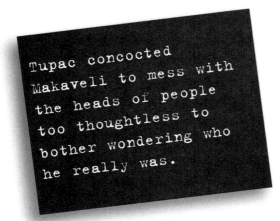

Tupac concocted Makaveli to mess with the heads of people too thoughtless to bother wondering who he really was.

If you know in this hotel room they have food everyday and I knock on the door. *Everyday* they open the door to let me see the party, let me see that they throwin' salami, throwin' food around but telling me there's no food. Everyday. I'm standing outside trying to sing my way in—'We are weak, please let us in. We are weak, please let us in.' After about a week that song is gonna change to 'We hungry, we need some food. After two, three weeks it's like, 'Give me some of the food! I'm breakin' down the door.' After a year it's like, 'I'm pickin' the lock, comin' through the door blastin'.' It's like 'I'm hungry!' you reached your level, you don't want any more, We asked ten years ago, we were askin' with the Panthers, we were askin' in the Civil Rights movement. Now those people who were askin' are all dead or in jail so what are we gonna do?"

And we shouldn't be angry! And the raps that I'm rapping to my community shouldn't be filled with rage? They shouldn't be filled with the same atrocities that they gave to me. The media they don't talk about it, so in my raps I have to talk about it, and it just seems foreign because there's no one else talking about it."

It's strange rhetoric for a successful man, but Tupac pumped himself up on it.

The disingenuousness in this interview makes it the most fascinating and revealing Tupac ever gave. Raised to see deprivation as the only Black reality, Tupac's complaint about success confesses the class envy most rappers hide:

> It's like bein' the last person alive. After three days you can't do anything. What can I do, where can I go? There's no Black neighborhood where Black people who have the same amount of money as me. There's richer and there's poorer. There's no just, you know "I did a movie, got a little bit of money, livin' OK' Black neighborhood, so I gotta live in a white neighborhood. I don't fit it, so that's hell. It's hell when you can't be around your peers. All my life I grew up around Black people, poor people. But I can't live around poor people now cuz they'll rob me. And why would they rob me? Because they're starvin', cuz there's no money here. But they telling me now that I've made a little money, I have to move here.

"Here" was Sherman Oaks, where Tupac had bought a home for his mother; located on the other side of Beverly Hills. It was the upscale suburb many in the Death Row stable had moved into—out of Long Beach, out of the ghetto—a place that signified some degree of affluence and attainment. But not a place where Tupac felt at home. For an ex-Panther and her children, Sherman Oaks represented dislocation and entrapment in a way that few understood.

"No one's ever trying to deal with this section," he said. "They're just movin' away from it and we're gonna have more stars comin' from the ghetto and they're gonna all move this way." This has no connection to the political ideas Tupac was weaned on. As Makaveli, he attempts to resolve his conflict between politics and showbiz solely on impulse. Tupac always said "People who think I'm like two different people—a wild gangsta and a caring, sensitive young black man—don't really know me." They failed to recognize that everyone shows aspects of themselves at different times to different people. Acting on

Machiavelli's popular saying "The end justifies the means" (derived from his play *The Prince*), Tupac concocted Makaveli to mess with the heads of people too thoughtless to bother wondering who he really was.

There are clues throughout *All Eyez on Me*: His ambition to rise above "jealous motherfuckers;" his hot sense of friends vs. enemies—and most of all, his speculation on a posthumous identity where "Only God Can Judge Me." On the song "When We Ride," Tupac equates Makaveli with American political foes but fans didn't pick up on the message. Given Tupac's many conflicts, it only resulted in confusion and mystery.

"ART IS NOT A SEPARATE ACTIVITY, IN ITSELF OR FOR ITSELF: IT IS A SOCIAL ACTIVITY, A TECHNIQUE OF LIVING, A HANDICRAFT IN FACT."

The Makaveli album, *The Don Killuminati The 7 Day Theory*, doesn't give an exact answer. It's an incomplete statement; at first it seems a mistake in progress, starting off with the kind of fabricated news broadcast Public Enemy made into an art form (and that Tupac imitated on *Me Against the World*). This one is a bulletin of label wars, a sea of confusion that Tupac, like Jonah, is trying to swim through.

"Hey-Yea!" Tupac sings at one point during "I Bomb First (my second reply)." It's the only joyous sound he ever put on record, yet he seems bugged, perhaps high (on mayhem). Since joining Death Row something awful had taken hold of his aesthetic: a new joy in fighting people as powerless as himself. Hiphop's good times were far behind Tupac now (Harry Allen had situated his growth as "on the cusp of Public Enemy's decline and N.W.A.'s rise"), and he is sinking into vitriol. His new vision (*Some say the game is all corrupted/ Fuck this shit*") is stated as a prayer on "Hail Mary."

As Makaveli, Tupac assumes his nastiest characterization yet. It's a persona game, like the imp, Gemini, that Prince introduced on "Partyman." But there's no balance between Tupac's street vision and moral vision. It's unsettling because, as Leopold Senghor described Negro culture, "Art is not a separate activity, in itself or for itself: it is a social activity, a technique of living, a handicraft in fact." Tupac had always believed in hiphop's function as a poetic description of the ways Black people live. Paula Giddings got close to Tupac's rationale when she examined the work of sixties street poet Don L. Lee:

> It is through this 'technique of living' that Lee hopes to redefine herohood in the black community. For he remembers his childhood heroes in the Black Bottom section of Detroit, where he grew up. They were the pimps and the pushers—black people who exercise some control over their environment and their lives. But in the final analysis their effect was negative to the community. So Lee frequently writes about those who have benefitted the community while he himself exercises an almost Ghandian self-discipline.

Makaveli's interest in stepped-up violence, portraying hostility as the nature of Black existence, illustrates the futility Tupac felt. "Toss It Up," one of the album's better tracks, rips off Blackstreet's "No Diggity." It's always good to hear that organ riff again—even distilled into itchy synthesized noises. But the technique is used nihilistically: "*We untouchable!*" he screams, alluding to Death Row's new label description, now used to replace "Out da Gutta." But also claiming invincibility. There ought to be some sense made of all this in "To Live and Die in L.A." It is an assessment, of sorts, a tribute to the good and bad ways of living in the city of angels. Yet throughout the album Tupac keeps falling back into ghetto meanness, brazenly mocking the kind of call-in radio shows his fans follow: a female radio DJ asks callers "This is Street Signs. How do you feel when you hear a record like Tupac's new one? Don't you feel like that creates tension between East and West? He's talking about killing people. . . I had sex with your wife—not in those words . . . he's talking about 'I want to see you deceased!'"

That's more like what Naughty By Nature's Treach actually said after Tupac's death on "Street Soldiers," Lisa Evers' rap show on New York's HOT-97 . "People who think Tupac deserved to die should die!" Treach was defending Tupac's memory but he, too, lacks cunning; as Brother O.P.P. he continues the animosity that brought Tupac grief in the first place.

Makaveli is a mythic figure conjured to justify the same illogic; he promises *"We may fight amongst each other but I tell you this: We burn this bitch down [if you] get us pissed."* It's a gangwar anthem for street soldiers without a strategy.

Prior to the release of *The Resurrection*, the Geto Boys had their own internal friction (less publicized than Tupac's feuds with Biggie Smalls and Sean Puffy Combs). In one of the greatest moments on *The Resurrection*, the ridiculous nature of hiphop squabbles is put into perspective:

```
        It's GB and Willie D reunited
      Sendin' niggas back to the studio
          To get they shit tighter
     The folks said it wouldn't happen again
 But we sat down and settled our differences like men
 And if that sounds too namby-pampy, Willie D talks even
                 plainer:
         We put the bullshit behind us
      Cause fuckin' up money ain't a plus
              It's a minus
```

Tupac could have learned from Geto Boys, *"the ultimate good of brotherhood."*

But Makaveli has little time for brotherhood. He capitalizes on the unfunny viciousness of the vaunted game "the dozens"—though it's good to hear Tupac put Nas in his place:

Think he live like me
Talk about he left the hospital
Takin' five like me
You livin' fantasies nigga
I reject yo deposit
We shoot Dre's punk ass
Now we out of the closet.

Those clever words most impress listeners who probably have no sense of urban Black revolutionary poetry that made its effect civilly, before it was a million-dollar safe bet. It's worth knowing what Don L. Lee (Haki Madhubuti) knew about Black art, as Paula Gidding put it in her 1971 study of Lee ("From a Black Perspective"): "That which does not edify black survival tends to nullify it."

One result is what Tupac considers "Blasphemy." The track with that title isn't really anti-religious; it's anti-reality. *"Have you ever seen a crackhead? That's eternal fire." "Mama, tell me, am I wrong? Is God just another cop waiting to beat my ass if I don't go pop?" "They say Jesus is a kind man but he should understand . . . I hope God can see my heart is pure."* All these suggestions go against good sense notions of living such as Geto Boys achieve on their album, which better suggests the chastened despair of genuine conversion Tupac was after but never managed to find.

Humility ought to be behind all this trash talk but, in what seems like an improvised process of recording this album, Tupac can't risk tenderness until he wears down his vapidity. The shift occurs with a clever duel between bass guitar and mandolin on "Life of an Outlaw"—a duel between gruffness and sweetness. *"It's hard to be a man running with my guns in hand,"* go the lyrics. But while "the gun in hand" falsifies, the musical instruments are the great persuaders. The musicians know more than the rapper about the values at stake in hiphop's moral dilemmas.

On "Just Like Daddy," Makaveli assumes a patriarchal role. Tupac and his crew rap bedroom endearments as though the only time they feel responsible to sisters is when they're sexing them. He's circled a long time around this raw realization of what constitutes manhood. And though it's a naively primal notion, at least it's a sign Tupac's finally paying attention to something outside his own body.

It's in the daddy role that Makaveli seems most traditional, still presuming male authority—as if Afeni had struggled for nothing. "Just Like Daddy" is the wishful promise of a boy longing for Daddy rather than a man pledging his commitment. To have wound up at this stage of parental envy says a lot about Tupac's personal confusion, but it also limits the love raps in "Just Like Daddy"—fervent, descriptive and plentiful though they are—to sexual illiteracy—more gender division and regressed priorities.

Having gotten this low, on "Krazy" Tupac blisses out and visions start to materialize:

Made a lot of money/ Seen a lot of places
And I swear I seen a peaceful smile on my mama's face
When I gave her the keys to her own house
'This yo land
Yo only son done became a man'

That's about as good as Don L. Lee ever was. These lines ring autobiographic the same way as "Dear Mama," with a more completely realized pathos. This is the post-jail album *All Eyez on Me* was too rushed to be.

How can a son of revolution, who means well, be so misguided? It's a bigger question than Tupac himself could answer. But the truth may lie in the confusions of race and class that Tupac and the people who loved him will not see through. The same rough themes are burdened by his limited stock of emotions.

It's the new sense of profit, admitting he got a little something out of the system besides grief, that makes the apologetic "Krazy" such a humane recitation.

My big mouth.
My big mouth.
I got a big mouth

Rash young listeners may thrive on Tupac's invective; older and more thoughtful listeners may share his disgust but back off from the songs themselves because they depict such a cramped way of thinking. A critical response to Tupac has to push past the easy instinct to simply regret the waste of talent. Fans who are comfortable pining for Tupac do a disservice to themselves, hobbling their own capacity to cope with the world, settling in to the confusion that only got Tupac nowhere—unable to reconcile the mixed-up human legacy that was left to him. Pop doesn't have to be this thick-witted to be passionate; much of it bursts with vitality while still offering a fine scrutiny of life's complications.

When asked what he was best known for, Tupac gave an encompassing answer:

My big mouth. My big mouth. I got a big mouth. I can't help it, I talk from my heart, I'm real. You know what' I'm sayin'? What ever comes, comes. But it's not my fault. I'm trying to find my way in the world. I'm trying to be somebody instead making money off everybody, you know what I'm sayin'? So I go down paths that haven't been traveled before. And I usually mess up, but I learn. I come back stronger. I'm not talkin' ignorant. So obviously I put thought into what I do. So I think my mouth and my controversy. I haven't been out of the paper since I joined Digital Underground. And that's good for me cuz I don't want to be forgotten. If I'm forgotten then that means I'm comfortable and that means I think everything is OK.

We can't forget the complicated, grateful/sorry part that money plays in Tupac's warped vision. Even though he forgets what James Brown knew: *"Money won't change you/ But time will take you on."* During the eighties Republican revolution a white pop band, The Brains, misread the signs and made "Money Changes Everything," a critically acclaimed record that defied Brown with the dream of the acquisitive. Black culture with it's feet on the ground used to know better. Tupac, in his angry delirium, behaved as if decades of Black perseverance and wisdom had taught him nothing. He thought change could be brought about by swaggering, pseudo-political exhortations, but he left Black depression exactly where it was before.

Tupac also said he was best known for:

> . . . taking five bullets. Surviving, I'm known as a survivor now, I hope so. For the jail thing, bullets and everything, controversies and everything. I hope so, and I want, in the future, I want people to be talking about me like, "You know, 'Remember when he was real bad? Remember when Tupac was real bad? Everybody changes, everybody becomes better people. We all should get that chance. I just want my chance.

Makaveli's final track, "Against All Odds" leads back to nowhere—Black antagonism. And you know how that ends. The line, *"Last words to a bitch nigga, why you lie?,"* are some of the last words Tupac ever recorded. When he rasps them out, his voice is tight. It doesn't bear the pain the way a gospel veteran like Pop Staples or a Southern rapper like Brad (Scarface) Jordan does. Makaveli's voice is clenched with urban tension, which makes that line reverberate back at him and his listeners. Will Tupac's death make a difference in the way rappers and fans confuse money love with the race bravado? Can grief lift them out of their dog-eat-dog narcosis? The rivalry between Tupac and Puffy, Dre, Biggie, Nas and Mobb Deep is unimportant next to the tension that encloses them all. Crabs in a barrel. One more rapper misunderstood. One more Black man in a box.

CHAPTER 17
"your entertainment, my reality"

will tupac be remembered as a stereotype or as his own man? Money B, who knew Tupac when, understood these pressures:

> The media, they all say, 'Gangster rapper Tupac, blah, blah, blah..' But if you knew Tupac, he was real sensitive, real intelligent, real political. You know, if you had a deep conversation with him, he'd get off into some deep shit wit'chu. But at the same time, don't try to play him. You know what I'm saying? He could go there. . . So the thing with 'Pac and the media is, the media never wants to know you. They wanna find something to jump on and run it. You know how it is.

But most hiphop fans don't know. Eager to find their culture—their lives—validated in the media, they have accepted its distortion both in reporting and

Tupac Shakur, July 5, 1994, spitting in the direction of reporters as he leaves state Supreme Court in New York.

in the industry-controlled making of hiphop.

When Tupac told *The City Sun* "We need to report our own truth," he spoke for the growing awareness among rappers that media untruths must be challenged. That's why Poppa LQ, a young rapper from Houston, chose *Your Entertainment, My Reality* as the title of his 1996 debut album: to announce the strain felt by Black American males in this period of intense media scrutiny and dwindling political sympathy. The slogan applies as much to the rapper's exploited role in the music industry as to the growing confusion in the media between sociopolitical news and entertainment, all too often starring Black folks in an ongoing saga of pathos and transgression. Civilians become performers. Performers become celebrities. Celebrities become criminals. Word becomes bondage. In what they say in their own defense, or what journalists say to manipulate the public's perception, an individual can be glorified or demonized, exonerated or judged guilty.

Tupac's reality became public entertainment in the era's ultimate stage show—the courts. And he played to it in a number of court cases that reality-checked his wild-entertainer antics. Unfortunately Tupac's infractions are rarely seriously considered by the mainstream as the result of plain old bad judgement or sheer bad luck. Only a hiphop publication like Long Island's *The Agenda* would dare to reason, "The only 'ignorant thing' Tupac may have done is used fk'd up judgment and made some ill-self-advised decisions. He, unlike a lot of other 'brothas', has been open about his deep love for niggas."

A repetition of the demonizing pattern has become a hiphop rite of passage— the mug shot replaces the headshot of young Hollywood hopefuls. This is how the mainstream media constructs demeaning views of hiphop stars. "That's bullshit, they gonna erase that gun out of my hand!" Tupac had said in 1990 when Paramount Pictures turned the airbrush on advertisements for *Juice*. The incident stayed with him as an example of how media constructs and "corrects" its images. Even critiques of Tupac's own art have been used as part of the distortion.

"Easy Target" is *Rolling Stone's* obituary piece. Written by Mikal

Gilmore, it represents the rock-crit establishment's old guard fear and loathing of hiphop. Implicit in the essay is the assumption that Black street talk exemplifies some intense, primal hatred and hostility. Gilmore takes "Hit 'Em Up" literally as Tupac's threat on the lives of anyone who's down with the East Coast—as if that might even include the staff of *Rolling Stone*. There's no room in Gilmore's reading of "Hit 'Em Up" for the possibility that a Black artist has enough cunning to pretend anger in a performance. In addition to dragging out tired out Staggerlee stereotypes to parlay Tupac's death into rock-n-roll copy, this pandering deliberately ignores the clear, intricate artifice of rap braggadocio.

Yet there *is* something new in "Hit 'Em Up" in terms of adding levels of vitriol and ingenuity to pop's proverbial "answer" record. Tupac made the track to address his suspected attackers in the infamous 1994 ambush; he follows the same below-the-belt strategy Roxanne Shante used that year in her no-sisterhood throw down "Big Mama." Female rappers Isis, Salt'N Pepa, MC Lyte, Queen Latifah, Monie Love and YoYo, who Shante suspects stole her thunder, all get dissed in a mean but spirited fashion. (*"Niggas came in flocks/ For blocks and blocks and blocks/ To watch the Rox/ Knock the bitches out the box."*) Shante's little-girl voice took infectious, juvenile glee in talking dirty. She flung shade through imaginative rhymes and jokey invective that Tupac, in "Hit 'Em Up," repeats but with a very male substitution of physical violence for metaphorical devastation.

As rap rivalry goes, "Hit 'Em Up" is an inferior answer to The Notorious B.I.G.'s "Who Shot Ya?," itself a B-side riposte, released after Tupac suggested Biggie Smalls and Sean "Puffy" Combs were involved in the 1994 shooting. This battle of the MC's was as much macho animus as a contest of artistry. Although Tupac hurled a high level of cuss words and explicit intimidation, for anyone interested in the art of rap, the ball clearly remained in Biggie's corner .

A master of sly slaughter, Biggie showed how lyrical language can be made to thrill and kill:

"Fuck all that bicker and beef

I can hear sweat tricklin' down your cheek."

AP Photo/Venue Bernardo-Prudhomme

Christopher Wallace (a.k.a. Biggie Smalls of Notorious B.I.G.) and Sean "Puffy" Combs leave a party at the Peterson Automotive Museum in Los Angeles on March 8, 1997, shortly before Wallace was shot to death.

Biggie, of course, wrote "Warning," containing some of the most subtle and audacious lyrics in all of pop: *"There's gonna be a lot of slow singin' and flower bringin'/If my burglar alarm starts ringin.'"* On "Who Shot Ya?" Biggie had already announced *"I feel for you like Chaka Kahn/ I'm the Don/ Pussy when I want/ Rolex on the arm/ You'll die slow but calm/ Recognize my face/ So there won't be no mistake/ So you'll know where to tell Jake/ Lame nigga/ Brave nigga/ Turned Front-Page Nigga.*" Aiming these sharpened thrusts, Biggie trumps like a cultural impresario, conjoining Chaka Khan's Black pop totem to his sarcasm, while his backing vocalists ruthlessly mock Tupac's five bullet wounds ("*We proceed to give you what you need*").

The only Tupac lyrics Gilmore quotes—and at length—is "Hit 'Em Up's" vituperation: "*You want to fuck with us, you little young-ass motherfuckers?. . . You better back the fuck up or you get smacked the fuck up . . . We ain't singin' we bringin' drama . . . We gonna kill all motherfuckers. Fuck Biggie, fuck Bad Boy . . . And if you want to be down with Bad Boy, then fuck you, too . . . Die slow, motherfucker.*"

To this Gilmore exclaims:

> I have never heard anything remotely like Tupac Shakur's breathless performance on this track in all my years of listening to pop music. [He must have missed Chuck D's "Live and Undrugged" and Johnny Rotten's "No Feelings."] It contains a truly remarkable amount of rage and aggression—enough to make anything in punk seem flaccid by comparison. Indeed 'Hit 'Em Up' crosses the line from art and metaphor to real-life jeopardy. On one level, you might think Shakur was telling his enemies: We will kill you competitively, commercially. But listen to the stunning last 30 seconds of the track. It's as if Shakur were saying: 'Here I am—your enemy and your target. Come and get me, or watch me get you first.

Gilmore should know better than to take such trash talk to heart or to suggest the ominous role of Biggie and Bad Boy Productions in Tupac's murder. Gilmore doesn't explain the intensified rivalries of East Coast-West Coast hiphop factions that turned teenage tribal spats into entertainment—a bad corporate joke on the smaller stakes of real life street gangs. Such writing only feeds lurid, racist suspicions. The blunt, unimaginative threats of "Hit 'Em Up" stand out to conventional music editors like a street mugging—a perfect opportunity to editorialize.

Geeked-up on Black "rage and agression," Gilmore wasn't listening very closely to "Hit 'Em Up." He missed the track's circular background mantra—*"Get money!"*—that exposed Tupac's intention to hew closely to the line of caustic but lucrative performance—the guiding aesthetic principle of gangsta rap. (Junior Mafia's "Get Money" is one of the signature hiphop releases of the age—Barrett Strong's bastard child.) These showbiz-reel life challenges dramatized disc waste the youthful ingenuity that hiphop at one time applied to African-American history and political strife. Now it's used (and validated in the mainstream press) to exaggerate dancefloor/Jeep competitions.

That's still where the battle is won.

Despite this rivalry, brotherhood was displayed when it counted—on *One Million Strong*, the Million Man March tribute album, Tupac and Biggie are united for a cause. Their track, "Runnin," resolves all petty feuds, giving hope to the possibility for rappers to come to their senses, to understand that unity in the face of Black social needs is more important than industry-sponsored pissing contests.

"Runnin'" survives from an earlier period—August 1994—before bad blood flowed between Tupac and Biggie. Tupac issued an official "no comment" about the song's inclusion on the *One Million Strong* album, but Biggie put the ironic track into focus when he told a reporter, "I support any brother who wants to move in the direction of more responsibility to our unity. We're all trying to get paid. Anything else is just bullshit." The terms of Tupac's rivalry with Bad Boy Entertainment coarsened what had been a healthy competition in hiphop.

Of the many essays written after Tupac's death, most are like coatracks on which writers hang their favorite theories. Two exceptions: Darryl James in *Rap Sheet* and Harry Allen, writing in *Rap Pages* brought the most knowledge and sensitivity to the subject without breaking down into maudlin excuses or valedictions. James provides an analogy to Marvin Gaye's "divided soul," based on the generosity of sentiment fans displayed, calling local Los Angeles radio station 92.3 The Beat which set up a hotline to "handle the calls of fans who did not know who to talk to or what to do, but found it difficult to process the death." The Gaye comparison fits with the communal sympathy in Rev. Daughtry's eulogy that expressed Black-American religious thinking (Daughtry's Jonah and the Whale parable fit popular notions of the rapper and the music biz behemoth with a moral perspective).

Allen's emotional flow stanched rumors of Tupac's resurrection and brought in telling details of Tupac's guiltlessness—as when misread stage directions at the 1995 *Source* magazine awards show led to 'Pac and his crew bumrushing A Tribe Called Quest's moment of glory.

In his passion for Tupac and the entire misread hiphop culture, Allen also gave a hint of Tupac's emotional life. "Like the love depicted in Shakespeare's *Romeo & Juliet*, the classic play he adored, he too was verboten, forbidden, and so pure and undiluted that the world itself could not stand him." That's Allen grieving—overcome rather than overstanding. But the *Romeo & Juliet* comparison is acute; it works as an indication of Tupac's exploitation. Angela Briggins, a student with Tupac at BSA, remembers him reading *Romeo & Juliet* with Jada Pinkett and Tupac later enthusing about one of her lines. "*Oh I have bought the mansion of a love/ But not possessed it/ And though I am sold/ Not yet enjoyed.*"

As a youngster those lines must have clicked for Tupac, describing how he felt believing in the Panther ideas he was taught but did not yet benefit from. (The verse also evokes the "love" Suge Knight offered with Death Row, love that Tupac bought but never lived to enjoy.) The romanticism Shakespeare evoked for Tupac fit an optimism in early hiphop that came to be at odds with the spirit of the nineties.

Fifties pop culture showed a better understanding of youth's tragic predicament when three Broadway hands—Arthur Laurents, that Panther sympathizer

Leonard Bernstein, and Stephen Sondheim—updated Shakespeare's exploration of cultural antagonism in *West Side Story* to address American class issues—the ruin of love by poverty and racism. As Gregory Solman points out, Baz Luhrmann's latest, degraded version of *Romeo & Juliet* avoids Shakespeare's point about a society that uses its children as chattel. This is the necessary truth virtually every Tupac memorial has avoided. It requires too painful a look at how even loving fans and rich executives got high off Tupac's blood.

But mostly the postmortems have continued the media assassination that hiphop has fended off from its beginning. And it still threatens to engulf Tupac's legacy in confusion. dream hampton had at Tupac again in several obits, her infatuation turned necrophilic. You wonder: how could a supposedly socially responsible media conspire to have hiphop chronicled by writers so insensitive that they print "Having attended dozens of funerals for young Black men in the past ten years, most of us must admit a certain numbness to violent death."

The after-death notice hampton did for *Rap Pages* reads:

> **And while, like a lot of women across the country, I was reduced to heaving sobs for the loss of Tupac Amaru Shakur, what's settled in its place is the calm that comes when one has completed an incredibly suspenseful novel. A sigh of relief is breathed; finally the drama—the roller coaster ride—is over.**

This is so distant from the difficult facts of life, it's no wonder hiphop fans and artists who take such writing as a clue to how the culture can be experienced, end up relying on fantasies, half-truths, nonsense and pseudo-politics.

Pearl Cleage repeatedly worries, "I'm too old to be writing about Tupac Shakur. My daughter made me do it." But what's worse is her ignorance about aspects of Black living that this event should have clarified.

> **I grew up with the Civil Rights Movement, the Vietnam War, Women's Liberation. I know what struggle is and I accept the inevitability of conflict, but**

I don't understand what it feels like to risk your life walking down the streets of your own neighborhood. I don't know how it feels to live a statistic . . .

This is no help; it could be the result of hiphop not breaking through to some intellectuals but a writer should be able to recognize the pieces of experience that are left out of certain artistic scenarios. Boys who bluff "Back up off me" are not rampaging egotists; life teaches you those bluffs are methods of staving off fear. In sentimentalizing Tupac's tragedy, writers neglect what they ought to know based on other art or their own lives. Cleage nostalgically recalls: "One big difference is we knew who the enemy was," implying the sixties' sense of the government-as-enemy but forgetting the competitive nature of society that expects, provokes, and condones cultural opposition—boys against boys, men against women, white against black, rich against poor.

The urban reality of anarchic violence isn't new. Without the basic sense of civility to notice everyday killing and brutality, all the "Stop the Violence" pomposity will get nowhere. Cleage reverts to sentiment when she says :

I am not in the habit of lusting after convicted sexual abusers just because they also happen to be charismatic, musical geniuses. Miles Davis broke me of all that, but I never thought Miles could be saved. Tupac was different. He seemed to be crying for salvation, struggling for clarity, searching for sanity in a world clearly gone mad.

When Cleage separates Davis' sins from Tupac's, she fails a clear-headed analysis of the patriarchy that binds them.

Sanyika Shakur, writing from prison, brings intelligence to Tupac's legacy but can't resist the eulogistic romanticism of saying "Tupac was a rider, a courageous young brother, and a street soldier." Shakur then forgets to distinguish between those roles. It's as bad as R.J. Smith writing in *Spin* that Tupac "went out like a champ." But Shakur knows better when he says:

> **In all honesty [Tupac] did tend to buzz about as if he alone were privy to some deep secret that would soon unveil itself. However, upon closer examination of his material and indeed his actions, it would appear that he was just in tune to the maniacal machinations of this menacing society.**

This, too, may be an excuse, but at least its an insightful one with the force of truth.

The legacy is more shoddily attended in the mainstream press—even by Black writers. Veronica Chambers apes dream hampton's smitten monkeyshines; in a tearful Tupac Lives! fantasy, she meets Mr. Makaveli in his hideout in Cuba—every radical's ideal tropical hangout. This tabloid fever dream isn't the only example of bad taste at *Esquire*; In a report on Tupac's last night in Las Vegas, *Esquire* indulges the same grisliness as *Spin* magazine when noting the Thug Life abdomen tattoo, then speculating on how surgeons cut into it. Even Chambers exploited Tupac as much as possible, supplying *Esquire* with dirt:

> **Tupac had a hard time following rules. Half the time there were no problems at all, but it wasn't unusual for Tupac to get high in his trailer, to be hours late to the [*Poetic Justice*] set in the morning, or to get pissed off for what seemed like no reason at all. Once, toward the end of the shoot, Tupac was told he could have a day off. That morning, the producers decided that they would shoot publicity stills and called Tupac to the set. He arrived with his homeboys and began screaming, 'I can't take this shit. Y'all treat a nigga like a slave.' He stormed off to his trailer and promptly punched in a window.**

Chambers had made no effort to understand this behavior when she was writing the promotional "making-of" book for *Poetic Justice*. But after Tupac's death, she lets the dirt fly:

> **At the time, nobody knew how far he was willing to take his mantras about**

living a "Thug Life." (Though Chambers never reminds *Esquire* how far Hollywood took its apprehension by forbidding John Singleton to cast Tupac in *Higher Learning*.) There was indignation on the set about being blasted by some young punk, but there was also fear; fear both *of* Tupac and *for* Tupac. I believe this was a pattern of concern that those around him felt right up until his death."

Most of the media's Tupac legacies amount to cruel dissections—but not helpful ones. The *New York Times* put stereotypical myth into the record. A front page headline read:

```
TUPAC SHAKUR, 25, RAP PERFORMER
WHO PERSONIFIED VIOLENCE, DIES.
```

At least Tupac, as a money-making star, got more respectable treatment from the *Times* than did Huey P. Newton who had the bad style to die on the same day as Diana Vreeland (So *Vogue*'s trendsetter got front page treatment while Newton was squeezed in the back pages). Jon Pareles' front page story blandly pronounced judgment as historical fact, calling Shakur "a rapper and actor who built a career on controversy," but that's from a disdainful point of view that ignores the charismatic emotional attraction that compelled listeners to actually buy records. There's more sense in his later paragraphs, "In some raps Mr. Shakur glamorized the life of the 'player'. . . he described gangsterism as a vicious cycle, a grimly inevitable response to racism, ghetto poverty, and police brutality." But the transformation of "gangsta" into gangsterism slyly changes an ineffectual social aberration into a major crime.

Rap, more than any other cultural form, has exposed the condescension in journalism—no where more than in the *Village Voice*'s objectification of Black cultural stereotypes. The *Voice* made entertainment of Tupac's trials, running feverish speculations about his shooting and hospital release as the lead Music

Section story (meanwhile neglecting to review the simultaneous release of Scarface's solo album *The Diary*—an extraordinary musical work that is the model for the psychological expression Tupac openly imitated). Tupac became a favored rapper for hip journalists because he exemplified white negro fantasies more than other rappers—L.L., too sane; Chuck D, too political; Speech, too erudite; Geto Boys, not slick enough; De La Soul, too idiosyncratic.

In the *Voice's* special obit section Tupac was deemed THUG FOR LIFE and a coterie of wannabes held forth with the adolescent claim: "High school is such a fantasy world it provides the sole complete analogy to hiphop"—a way to infantilize Black artistry. For the *Voice*, the ubiquitous Tupac's death on Suge Knight while cutting into that tattoo again. Nelson George called Tupac a "tan DeNiro." Only Natasha Stovall managed some genuine reporting that included Rosie Perez's phone call to Monie Love's radio show:

> **Tupac was not a dark-sided man. He was a misguided man. And I think that we all have to take some responsibility for how he went down . . . I should have had more courage, been more patient with him, and said, "Listen you're not going to push me away, you're not going to go with these new friends. I'm going to keep telling you "No. I love you."**

Death doesn't change the mainstream press' attitude toward hiphop, it's still viewed as a dangerous, alien form. *Rolling Stone* and *Spin,* the nation's largest circulated pop music magazines regularly restrict hiphop acts on their covers. *Rolling Stone* posthumously lauded *All Eyez on Me* as "one of rap's few full-length masterpieces," then gave a severely biased, brief history of recent rap:

> **Rap began to report on and reveal many social realities and attitudes that most other arts and media consistently ignored—that is, rap gave voice and presence to truths that almost no other form of art or reportage was willing to accommodate. Works like N.W.A.'s "F——tha Police" and *Niggaz4Life* may**

Tupac Shakur with Chuck D.

have seemed shocking to some observers, but N.W.A. didn't invent the resentment and abuse that they sang about. Nor did Ice-T, Ice Cube or the Geto Boys invent the ghetto-rooted gang warfare and drive-by shootings that they sometimes rapped about.

Left out of that synopsis is Public Enemy, a rap group very much involved with "reporting" urban struggle and mayhem. Tupac made no secret of his love for Public Enemy's album *It Takes a Nation of Millions to Hold Us Back* but Public Enemy's political explanations have always been disapproved by the mainstream music press and so are left out of histories slanted towards a segregated view of American culture.

Absolution is the point of these articles—absolution for indifferent Americans but mostly for the fans, writers, and industry professionals who cossetted Tupac in support of the most destructive industry practices. *Rolling Stone* suggests "Death Row and Bad Boy could have a true and positive impact on Black American political life" assuming those companies and that life have nothing to do with white America. *Billboard* magazine editor Timothy White wrote a merciless editorial decrying Tupac and letting the biz off the hook.

In *Vibe* magazine absolution reached a particular low when Danyel Smith recalled cheering on Tupac's first taste of success—celebrating his new apartment, new couch, flatware, and a "cedar-colored" maid. Noticing guns on a glass-top coffee table, Smith acknowledges "The firearms sat like dried piles of shit—not stinking but still foul." Yet as the party went on, with Tupac literally acting out Scorsese's *Who's That Knocking at My Door* gunplay scene, the *Vibe* editor and friends indulged his recklessness. And that's the role the culture played in Tupac's death. Not stinking perhaps, but still foul.

CHAPTER 18
keeping it reel

against the many negative images, there are positive images in numerous music videos that Tupac made. Angela Briggins remembers watching video tapes of *Black Caesar* and *Superfly* with Tupac in Baltimore. "*Superfly* was funny but it didn't mean as much to him as *Black Caesar*, cuz that had a Black man thinking up ways to control his neighborhood and his destiny. Like in *Shaft*. Tupac liked those because the heroes took control."

TV pundits Siskel & Ebert once registered surprise that rappers made such good actors, but role-playing is a large part of what any recording artist does. It's especially important to rap stars. Tupac, looking for more acceptance, delighted:

Yeah, I like that people come to me and go '*you* did a good job,' when all my career it's been you guys this or that. I love it that somebody come and say 'Tupac, you a great actor, you did a great part.' So now I want to do that even more and do other parts and do better parts. I want to do *Terminator 2* roles, something different so people can really see the diversity cuz even now people, I think some people,

goin' 'Now wait a minute, that's just him being him. How hard is it to be crazy?' Now I want to do something, you know, sane. I want to be in love or something so that people can see the diversity of what I can do.

Tupac Shakur and Mickey Rourke at the Benefit for San Salvador.

Rose Hartman/Globe Photos

His last two film productions were aimed in that direction. In *Gang Related*, a courtroom drama by writer-director Jim Kouf, Tupac stars with James Belsushi, Lelila Rochon and, in small cameo parts, James Earl Jones and Dennis Quaid. Belushi and Tupac are partners, corrupt homicide detectives, who get involved in shady stuff and chalk it up to gang-related activity—the usual formula. But *Gridlock'd*, Tupac's first independent film, is another story. Written and directed by the actor Vondie Curtis Hall, *Gridlock'd* is credibly based on Hall's real life experience of trying to get help and find his way through the big city bureaucracies of drug clinics and rehabs. As members of a spoken-word trio, Tupac (as Spoon), Tim Roth (as Stretch), and Thandie Newton (as Cookie), play Detroit junkies who make a desperate effort to go straight, all the while facing inevitable death with gallows humor. "You ain't gonna die, it's just a flesh wound," Tupac says to Roth after a shooting. The line has eerie echoes; it works as part of a story which doesn't trade on Tupac's personal woes but paints a gritty portait of urban reality, satirizing the simplistic political notions of a dead-end society. In a bold move for a first-time Black filmmaker, Hall breaks with Hollywood fantasy conventions, choosing a documentary style that manages to avoid all the pitifalls of TV-series realism.

Roth's appearance brings to mind *Meantime*, the signal eighties BBC film about life on the dole that he made with English director Mike Leigh. Roth's impressive British technique meshes with Tupac's naturalism, making them a good team. He remembers their working relationship fondly:

> **My mate-name for Tupac was 'New Money,' because he was the upstart, full of the esprit of being a big pop record star and he was certain to be a smashing film star. He used to call me 'Free Shit' because of the extra perks he thought I got in my dressing room, trailer, what have you.**

Together, they avoided the hooey-quotient of actors getting high on playing druggies.

Gridlock'd deftly shifts dramatic tone from slapstick-comic (a welfare office riot) to horrific-comic (a hospital waiting room nightmare). Hall, who starred in the memorable eighties theater production *Williams & Walker* (about the moral crises felt by 1920s blackface performers Bert Williams and George Walker), lets the actors explore the complexities of good luck and bad breaks.

Tupac Shakur and Tim Roth in Gridlock'd.

Remembering Tupac, Hall said:

> When you think about George Walker and Bert Williams, they were complete-ly different individuals off the stage and 'Pac was a lot more stuff than he seemed when outside the rap arena. The producer Preston Holmes got him the script and he said 'I want to do this movie.' The brother showed up, he had the script down, had the characters arc. He could talk about the beats, he could make reference to all the shit. I thought, 'This is not the cat the media is throwin' out there.' He's smart, funny, well read.
>
> That's what saddened me about his death, you could see the compassion and silliness. In the media all you see is the picture with the hat skewed to the side, not even the pictures of what he was looking like when we were work-ing. Just a straight up Black man.
>
> I went to the memorial benefit his mother gave. Ex-Panther after ex-Panther spoke. When you talk to the folks 'Pac grew up around, you sensed why the brother was like that; sitting around with his mother's friends, having the revolutionary brothers have a dialogue at a table and sense his mothers spirit and brilliance. It was evident when he was on set. He could reference any shit, it was because he was around fuckin' intellectuals when he was born. [He had] a diverse taste in music, the guy pulls up the girl in The Cranberries. He knew every artist out there. All these films, all this music; he sort of absorbed all this stuff.
>
> One time when we were driving in L.A. in his Rolls Royce Corniche he had the Cranberries blaring. He was on Crenshaw Blvd. Some brothers pulled up, said 'Pac, what you listening to?' 'Just the radio,' he said. But it was the CD.

Hall appreciated Tupac's ecclectic qualities; he knew that actors, like rap-pers, when intuitively in sync, reveal their most poignant secrets. *Gridlock'd* marked the first time since *Juice* that Tupac had worthy collaborators who understood his pressures. Hall envisioned a trenchant hope, "Tupac's movie career could have brought out more sides of his personality, so that people could know him better."

Tupac had always wanted to act out revolution in real life. Years earlier, Explaining the meaning of THUG LIFE, his motto and tattoo, he had talked of a plan to start a camp for children on the order of L.L. Cool J.'s but with a militant purpose: to teach kids how to use firearms. Tupac had launched into an energetic proselytizing, full of race-war threats and mounting panic that only made sense as an expression of his own churning anxieties. As he spoke, and his fears uncoiled, he exuded more and more fanatical certainty.

It was this ambition and mood that inspired the movie-parody concept of the *California Love* video. Directed by Hype Williams, the hiphop video director who specialized in Hollywood knock-offs, Tupac was cast as an apocalyptic scavenger, modeled on characters in *The Road Warrior*. *California Love* exhibits his firebrand mania in images already accepted in pop culture. Though its source is trivial, Tupac embraced its form to validate his dream of apocalyptic action. Williams hypes it up with overlapping images and sped-up chases, disco fantasias, fight-scenes that have nothing to do with the song's lyrics—all of which totally contradict—and perhaps parody—his second, conventional video of the song set at a party in contemporary L.A. These compacted hiphop visions convey how hard it has become for young people to stabilize their passions and choose sensible paths. They're overflowing with feelings—emotions that need to be sorted out, examined, balanced, corroborated.

Rap Sheet editor Darryl James wrote of meeting Tupac and observing: "The Tupac who stood in front of me then was just a cool kid who was funny as hell and just wanted people to like him." That's the Tupac immortalized in *I Ain't Mad at Cha*, a video he co-directed that imagines his death by gunfire and his ascension to heaven where he greets Black pop stars from Billie Holiday and Redd Foxx to Jimi Hendrix and Sammy Davis, Jr., James remembers the hopeful young star who said "I never had shit growing up, so I had nothing to lose. Now I want to show what I've been through to other people who've been through the same thing, to show how narrowly I escaped. I stand up for something: I want to take the bad and turn it into good."

I Ain't Mad at Cha dramatizes Tupac's bonding with his homie (played by Bokeem Woodbine), shifting back and forth between heaven and earth so Tupac can keep an eye on his friend's reactions and see him being inspired by Tupac's death to keep on keeping on. It recalls another unexpected favorite film of his, Steven Spielberg's *Always*, in that love is so strong it keeps going beyond the grave. Tupac's theatrical instincts are shrewdly apparent in *I Ain't Mad at Cha*. The caring expressed in the video and it's link-up with the Black showbiz tradition is true to the kinds of sincerity and fraternity that hiphop revived for a new generation of Black pop fans.

Picking up on the song's message of forgiveness, Tupac's video dramatizes his longing for a bond with legendary Black pop stars. Looking past the egotism of this minidrama, it vividly depicts Tupac's desire to connect and identify with others who have left an "immortal" mark on the world through their achievement in the performing arts. It's significant that his heaven is not filled with political dissidents and rebels; the stress of Death Row had taken him beyond those factional concerns.

I Ain't Mad at Cha tells all those who had offered him political solutions that he has seen his own world and time in a different light. He has defined his personal struggle in new terms. In addition to being a Black American male—an endangered species—he is contending with the complications of being an entertainer, of standing with one foot in the system and one foot in the street, reaching for the very top. In the pursuit of artistic expression and a public career—in spite of compromises and obstacles—Tupac has found challenge and reward enough. The optimism of this video enacts Tupac's desire to transform his earthly struggle into a quest for enduring fame and lasting remembrance . . . for paradise and redemption.

Tupac rarely admitted this drive, preferring instead to speak through hiphop's usual bravado in which "keeping it reel" meant limiting himself to ghetto stereo-

MC Hammer, Snoop Doggy Dogg and Tupac Shakur join black activists group Brotherhood Crusade Thursday Aug. 15, 1996 in LA to kick off a campaign against the "Three strikes" law and to oppose the California Civil Rights Initiative, the anti-affirmative action measure.

types—what video director Mark Romanek calls "brick wall videos" that present hiphop performances in predictable slum settings. In *I Ain't Mad at Cha*, Tupac goes one step beyond cliche, daring to resist the "street" trend for a music video vision that brings him closer to an epiphany and closer to examining the hereafter alluded to in so many of his raps. Partly inspired by Bone Thugs-N-Harmony's *Tha Crossroads* video that spans the Black church to the afterlife, Tupac represented hiphop sentiments in a setting that might even have charmed Rev. Daughtry. Keeping it "reel" in this case meant an unusual effort to keep hiphop spiritual.

Video-making fully utilized Tupac's rap and dramatic ambitions. Lisa Steinberg recalled the hiphop faith he had shown in 1993 when Mac Mall, a struggling Bay Area rapper, needed a video to promote his single, "Ghetto Theme." "I played it for 'Pac," Steinberg remembers. "And he said 'I'm gonna be a director, so this is where I'm gonna start, with the video I'm gonna direct. You gotta let me.' Actually he didn't give us a choice." The chance to make images that expressed his feelings for life in the 'hood inspired Tupac. "I love the song," he said. "I feel it. This is my project." Putting his seal on a ghetto anthem—even on someone else's—showed Tupac's awareness of the importance of confirming hiphop's complicated experience. "Video's a signal," he said. "So you turn it up!"

I Ain't Mad at Cha envisions sorrow, remorse, and forgiveness, as clear and concise as Tupac would ever manage. The video's wishfulness may seem naive because of hokey directorial devices and low-budget scenery. But it suggests that, up to the time he adopted his alter ego Makaveli, Tupac sharpened his ambitions while he outraced his dreams.

AFTERWORD

This is a sad story, but it fits in with the complexity of love that survives in Black pop. To make the most sense of Tupac's life, there is need to attach it to the efforts of other contemporary Black artists who, similar to Tupac, struggle with the effort to achieve and survive. The fact that listeners love Tupac so much weighs immeasurably. And love may hide all faults, but criticism can't. Responding to Tupac's art fully, honestly, requires critical thinking because it's a response to a version of the world that one can either recognize or dismiss. It is, as a recent book of poems and essays about Tupac asserts, *Tough Love*.

Tupac's conflicts over morality, behavior, and politics reflect a familiar Black American dilemma—conflicts no caring person can disavow. Rappers are no different from other working people who try to rationalize their subservience to a system that wears them down, but the history of Blacks in pop music is complicated by the phenomenon of a people uniting the stress of hard labor with the enjoyment of a pasttime. What worked in Tupac's favor is that the recognition of these conflicts stems from something very personal, and universal: the struggle for a decent living. It's as radical as it is simple. And so, in search of answers to Tupac's death, I have pursued musical clues to his life.

They echo throughout American pop cultural history, in the legacies I got from my parents, my brothers, and my sisters, and my friends. I remember my own youthful excitement about the opening of the 1964 New York World's Fair being dampened by TV news broadcasting a boycott of picket signs and protests from the old Congress of Racial Equality. Why spoil a happy occasion? I asked my older brother. "Because they have to," he responded with an air of serious dedication. "They have to take whatever opportunity they can to get people to know the importance of what they believe in." Imperative glowed for me ever since, and it's not farfetched to imagine that glow lighting up Tupac's face as he told his future to Rev. Daughtry. It's for the good taste and caring such mentors showed me that, when I think of Tupac, the best thought I can come up with is mixed with the complexities of trust, disappointment, and love. Dialogue from *A Raisin in the Sun,* Tupac's first acting experience, sums it up—and it keeps my head ringing:

> **You feelin' like you better than he is today? Yes? What you tell him a minute ago? That he wasn't a man? Yes? You give him up for me? You done wrote his epitaph too—like the rest of the world? Well, who give you the privilege? There is always *something* left to love.**

Caught between affection and anger, Tupac's love songs are the clearest expression of hiphop's emotional morass. "Dear Mama" and "Papa'z Song" are, despite their bitterness, love songs—the only kind of love song a tormented young adult can muster. The young person who rages at the world so single-mindedly also struggles to honor his perplexing foundations and the guardianship that brought him to such a precarious position. At heart, it's a generational rift between Civil Rights Era self-esteem and hiphop era issues of dignity and independence. Each generation's indebtedness to its forbears' way of thinking and doing is subtly queried or alluded to in every hiphop art work.

This legacy includes William Gunn's great play *The Forbidden City*. Gunn, the filmmaker and actor best known for his script to *The Landlord* and his psychological vampire movie *Ganja and Hess*, was not an artist of the hiphop generation but *The Forbidden City's* premier on the day after his death in 1989 (the same year as De La Soul's 3 *Feet High and Rising* was released) resembled a passing-of-the-torch in Gunn's complexly imagined summation of Black survivalist wordplay and mind games.

Gunn's heroine, Miss Molly, reacts to the racist world of the 1930s with a hardened bravura that bewilders her husband and her one remaining son, Nick, Jr. In a bizarre echo of Afeni's own dejection, Miss Molly says, "Gumption seldom does colored men any good. It'll most likely get you killed." She remembers an infant son's death (a killing that recalls Bessie Smith's) and raps a warning soliloquy to Nick, Jr.:

That year five thousand Negro men had been lynched in North Carolina alone. At dawn, if you were sent on errands, you could find somebody's brother or daddy hanging in a tree. It was the men they wanted. Why? What have you done? Is it something I don't know about? Why do you die so much? They let David die because he was a boy. I know it. Because he was colored and because he was a boy? Why are they so afraid of you that they murder little boys? Why? I'm in a stew because you can't kill back. And it keeps me from lovin' you too much, in case they murder the both of you.

The speech churns with much of the same agony that animates hardcore hiphop. Miss Molly "Brings the pain" (to use Wu-Tang's phrase)—a personal assessment of race horror from slavery to the Atlanta child murders to contemporary police brutality. Gunn's tangled attempt to explore the consciousness of this legacy also shows up in Tupac's conflicted art—his ambivalence about his mother's failings and her own, undependable examples—on "Part Time Mutha" he cites contradictory parental behavior and advice. Gunn's connection to Tupac can be seen in hiphop's basically contrary nature that starts from the current generation's response to the idea of domestic and social discipline.

So many of the most devastating lines in rap (such as Public Enemy's deliberately twisted anagram "Ain't-how-that-God-planned-it?" from "Fear of a Black Planet?") have to do with questioning authority and its lessons. Such challenges vibrate with youthful gusto, but that relish can leave a rapper confounded. Songs like "Dear Mama" express a child's frustration with parental imperfection, thus, (as in Gunn's fevered drama) an impertinence towards history. Tupac's sea-change of brotherly values in the irresistibly rabble-rousing "Five Deadly Venoms" blocks the kind of commiseration with his forbears that can come with maturity, therapy or revelation. Ice-T made one of his best raps about "The Hunted Child," portraying the imperilled situation of young Black males dodging law and fate, but few rappers have honestly confronted hiphop's most characteristic figure: The Unhumbled Child.

Speculation on Tupac's distress assumes that he was on his way to enlightenment, close to a redemptive, loving vision of the whole world (the same wish favored about Malik Hajj El-Shabazz). But despite fan's fantasies, there are no short cuts on the road to Damascus and Tupac, apparently, was cut-off before he got to his. Rev. Daughtry recalls the distance Tupac displayed when he said "I have to write what I know about, what I have lived, I don't know anything about the church or religion." That was a part of his mother's discipline that the unhumbled child rejected. At the same time, it put distance between the rapper and that portion of Black compassion that is generated around the emotional warmth of the church—the public hearth in many working class cultures.

You can hear this ardor on Blackstreet's album *Another Level*. "Don't Leave Me" uses the same sample as "I Ain't Mad at Cha." In this production, the four young singers end the album's quest for everyday meaning with play-back answering-machine messages from their mothers. Something of Afeni's concern comes through, but it's stated from a fundamentally different principle than activism. There's obvious maternal adherence to Christian doctrine but what's extraordinary is the timbre of the women's voices. Each mother speaks in a personally-derived version of church lingo (*"God is able to do anything but fail. I'm prayin' for you and your group. Remember to put God first"*), but the tone of voice is distinctively instructive (*"I want you to think where God has brought you from; he has brought you a mighty long way"*); patient (*"I know one day will be back home after you finish singin' this rock and roll."*); kindly commending (*"You been through a hard time strugglin' through your career but you kept pressin' on you have been obedient you have don't never forget where you came from and don't forget what your father has taught you always remember to do good do right and be brave"*); and devoted (*"Teddy, you came a long way you went the wrong way then God see fit to put in my heart to bring you back the right way to tell you the right things to do and so far you have prospered through your music and God have blessed you through song and music through your heart through your fingers through your mind"*). They're all the mother's voices you carry in your head. To hear these women respond to their sons' success with the appropriate measure of gratitude and loving wariness, is overwhelming. These taped messages are redolent of the life's work of child-rearing. Care and mercifulness are the ideas that come across, extending the feelings on "Thank You For My Child" to the examples of how four sister souljahs deal with the awesome burdens of their children's success, fickle fortune, life itself.

"Motherlude" precedes Blackstreet's own *pro forma* spiritual, "The Lord is Real (Time Will Reveal)," a Take 6-style haut-pop-gospel, that manages to put forth the case of how a child is prepared for life by an elder's good example. These mothers have achieved their own transcendent social visions and are able to impart endurance and appreciation—not confusion.

The challenge to hiphop is to make the best use of the lessons history (and parents) hand down. Such a formidable task makes one react uncomfortably to Tupac's brash, ill-prepared rancor because that unhumbled child had ingested a defeatist message that brought him up short. Tupac's pragmatism needs to be properly understood as just a part of the philosophical spectrum that hiphop can follow. In its simplified forgiveness, "Dear Mama" reverses "Motherlude's" benediction yet, instead of revealing as much about what this generation of young men feel about life and obligation, it skips over the son's capacity for growth and faith. Not to blame Afeni's good efforts—a lesson taught also has to be learned—those gifts, plainly, were not imparted to Tupac and I want to present the side of the parent-child relationship that is possible in rap and is illustrated by still another poignant landmark of the hiphop era, R. Kelly's "I Believe I Can Fly."

Released after Tupac's death, "I Believe I Can Fly" puts emotional heft behind the Michael Jordan-Bugs Bunny live-action-plus-animation movie *Space Jam*—a jolly, lightweight celebration of Jordan's ascendance to the mainstream. But Kelly, tasting his own burgeoning success, does something special with the concept. Like Bone Thugs-N-Harmony, whose second release tempered heady fame with metaphysical reflection in "Tha Crossroads," Kelly gets deep by getting spiritually high. Taking the next, necessary step after gangsta rap's nihilism, Kelly's romantic singing develops his New Jack smoothness into gospel, a remarkable new hybrid even better than Take 6 or such uplifting power-pop as the Jennifer Rush/Celine Dion "The Power of Love" or Gloria Estefan's "If I Can Reach".

Kelly's previous hit single, "Down Low," featured him in a quasi-Tupac role as a sneak-thief lover; in a remix rendition, Kelly pulled out the stops for a breakthrough erotic groan. Yet the sensual extremes seemed more like a stunt than the natural fusing of sacred and profane ecstacy heard in Aretha Franklin's sixties classics. "I Believe I Can Fly" takes Kelly there because the song's subjects—faith, possibility—directly relate to the hiphop era's concern with justice,

Black potential, salvation-over-survival. Kelly's tremulous moans aren't merely orgasmic, but orgasm's correlative—the sound of a divine struggle. When he sings "*I believe I can soar*," the aural play on "sore" takes you back to the primacy of old Negro spirituals with their heaven-and-earth, pain-and-redemption multiple meanings. Kelly sets off a dynamic of moral sensitivities, the virtues instilled when a parent conveys that one's word is one's essence or that the help one gives others ennobles oneself. It's not a reversion, its hiphop reclaiming the sustenance Black folks used to get from gospel.

Tupac evaded the political, moral instruction that would have taught him to connect his suffering and struggle to a redemptive idea (in "Only God Can Judge Me" he seems to be citing religiosity by rote). But that does not mean redemption is impossible to speak of in hiphop. Tupac's agony comes from the limits people placed on how he should think, restrictions eventually put on the hiphop form itself. By making rap solely a report from the street, hiphop censors what there is of Black America's own (good) news. "Heaven Ain't Hard to Find" attempts agape yet prompts a secular refutation reminiscent of Ice Cube's skeptical "When I Get to Heaven." The song ends *All Eyez on Me* perhaps because it's what Tupac wanted to say at the time. But what he really wanted was to find significance in earthly pleasure, physical excitement, the cruel world met on crude terms.

Andrea Renault/Globe Photos

WORKS

DISCOGRAPHY

Tupac Shakur was just beginning to forge a career. Even this short list of record releases—all made within a six year period—is, for a hiphop artist, extensive and ambitious. Hollywood, of course, was late to catch-up, so the six movies listed merely scratch the surface of Shakur's rising charisma.

Singles and Albums
"Same Song," *This is an EP Release* (Digital Underground)—Tommy Boy 0964
Sons of the P (Digital Underground)—Tommy Boy 1045
The Body-Hat Syndrome (Digital Underground)—Tommy Boy 1080
2Pacalypse Now—Interscope 91767-4
"If My Homies Call," Bust It 2—Priority Records 3933-99458-2
Strictly For My N.I.G.G.A.Z. . . —Interscope 92209-4

"I Get Around," Maxi Single

"Keep Ya Head Up," Maxi Single

"Papa'z Song," Maxi Single

"Definition of a Thug Nigga," *Poetic Justice* Soundtrack—Epic EK 57131

"I Get Around," *Straight From Da Streets*—Priority Records 4992-53885-2

"I Get Around (Remix)," *MTV Party to Go* Volume 5—Tommy Boy 1097s

Thug Life Volume 1—Interscope 92360-2

"Cradle to the Grave," Maxi Single

"Pour Out a Little Liquor," *Above the Rim* Soundtrack

Me Against The World—Interscope 92399-2

"Dear Mama," Maxi Single

"Dear Mama," *MTV Party To Go* Volume 7—Tommy Boy 1138

"So Many Tears," Maxi Single

"Temptations," Maxi Single

"My Block," *The Show* Soundtrack—Def Jam 314 529 021-2

"Throw Your Hands Up," *Pump Ya Fist, Hip Hop Music Inspired by the Black Panther*—Avatar 69712 4048-2

"High 'Til I Die," *Sunset Park* Soundtrack—Flavor Unite/EastWest 61904-2

"Made Niggas," *Supercop* Soundtrack—Interscope 90088

"Me Against the World," *Bad Boys* Soundtrack—Work/Sony 67009

"Runnin'," *One Million Strong*—Mergela 72667

All Eyez On Me—Death Row/Interscope 314-524 204-2

"California Love," Single

"How Do U Want It," Maxi Single

"2 of Amerikkka's Most Wanted," Single

"Hit Em Up"/ "How Do U Want It?"—Death Row/Interscope 422-854 653-2

"Slipping into Darkness," *Day of the Dead* (Funky Aztecs)—Raging Bull Records 2011

"California Love," DJ Red Alert Presents

"California Love," *MTV Party To Go* Volume 10—Tommy Boy 1194

"So Many Tears," *Hip Hop's Most Wanted*

The Don Killuminati The 7 Day Theory—The New and "Untouchable" Death Row
  Records/Interscope 90039

"Smile," *The Untouchable*—Rap-A-Lot Records 7243 42799-2

"Wanted Dead or Alive," "Never Had a Friend Like Me," "Out the Moon (Boom. . .
  Boom. . . Boom)," *Gridlock'd*

Soundtrack—Interscope 06949

FILMOGRAPHY

Juice Directed by Ernest Dickerson, script by Gerard Brown. Paramount Pictures 1990

Poetic Justice Directed by John Singleton, script by Singleton. Columbia Pictures 1993

Above the Rim Directed by Jeff Pollack script by Pollack. New Line Pictures 1994

Gridlock'd Directed by Vondie Curtis Hall, script by Hall. Grammercy Pictures 1997

Bullet Directed by Julien Temple. Trimark Pictures 1997

Gang Related Directed by Jim Kouf, script by Kouf. Orion Pictures 1997

TIMELINE

The Life of Tupac Amaru Shakur

June 16, 1971	Tupac Shakur is born in New York University Hospital to Afeni Shakur and Billy Garland. Afeni Shakur, a member of the Black Panther Party, was released from jail only a month earlier on charges of conspiracy to bomb several public places in New York City. Billy Garland was not a part of Afeni Shakur's life at the time of Tupac's birth and had no contact with his son until almost twenty years later.
1971 to 1986	Tupac and Afeni lived in New York City moving often between the Bronx and Harlem and at different times residing in homeless shelters.
September 1983	Twelve year old Tupac Shakur joined a Harlem theater

group, The 127th Street Ensemble. In his first performance, he played Travis in Lorraine Hansberry's play, "A Raisin in the Sun".

1985	The Shakur family moved to Baltimore, MD, where Tupac enrolled in the Baltimore School for the Performing Arts. It is here where Tupac met his life-long friend and fellow star Jada Pinkett. He wrote his first rap lyrics and performed under the name of MC New York.
June 1988	Tupac is forced to leave school in Baltimore before graduating and move with his mother to Marin City, California.
August 1988	Tupac moved out of his mother's home and is soon selling drugs.
September 1988	Tupac's stepfather, Mutulu Shakur is sentenced to 60 years in prison for his involvement in a 1981 armored-car robbery.
1989	Tupac starts a short-lived rap group, Strictly Dope, with his friend Ray Luv, managed by agent Leila Steinberg and produced by Atron Gregory of TNT records.
1989	Tupac becomes chairman of The New African Panthers, an organization of black youth determined to honor the goals of the original Panthers without duplicating their mistakes.

Early 1990	Tupac joins rap group Digital Underground as a dancer and rapper.
January 1991	Tupac made his record debut with Digital Underground's "This is an EP Release" song entitled, "Same Song".
November 12 1991	Tupac's first solo album entitled, "2Pacalypse Now," is released and goes gold launching his recording career.
December 1991	Tupac files a $10 Million lawsuit against Oakland police for alleged brutality following an arrest for jay-walking.
January 17, 1992	Tupac makes his big screen debut in the Earnest Dickerson film "Juice" earning him praise for his portrayal of the character Bishop.
April 1992	Ronald Ray Howard, 19, shoots a Texas trooper and Howard's Attorney claims that Howard was incited by Tupac's album "2Pacalypse Now," which was in his tape deck at the time.
August 22 1992	Tupac has an altercation with some old acquaintances in Marin City which results in the death of a 6-year old bystander and the arrest of Tupac's half brother, Maurice Harding, who was eventually released due to lack of evidence.
February 1993	Tupac released his second solo album entitled, "Strictly for my N.I.G.G.A.Z.," which eventually went platinum,

surpassing the sales of his first album.

March 13, 1993	Tupac got into a fight with a limo driver who accused Tupac of using drugs in his car. Tupac was arrested but the charges were eventually dropped.
April 1993	Tupac was again arrested. This time for taking a swing with a baseball bat at a local rapper during a concert. He was sentenced to serve 10 days in prison.
July 23, 1993	John Singleton's "Poetic Justice" was released, in which Tupac plays Lucky, a young postal worker, alongside Janet Jackson.
October 31, 1993	Tupac is arrested for allegedly shooting at 2 off-duty Atlanta police officers who were allegedly harassing black motorists. The charges were dropped.
November 18, 1993	A 19 year old woman accuses Tupac of sexual assault.
March 10, 1994	Tupac begins serving a fifteen day prison sentence for punching director Allen Hughes after he was dropped from the motion picture "Menace II Society."
March 23, 1994	Tupac appears in the movie, "Above the Rim," where he plays a troubled drug dealer. The soundtrack which features the song, "Pour Out A Little Liquor," recorded by Tupac's group, Thug Life, sells over 2 million copies.
September 7, 1994	Two Milwaukee teens murder a police officer and cite

	Tupac's song entitled "Souljah's Story" as their inspiration.
November 1994	Tupac's sexual assault trial opens.
November 30, 1994	Entering the lobby of the Quad Recording Studios in Times Square, New York City, Tupac is shot 5 times and robbed of jewels and cash estimated to be worth over $50,000.
November 31, 1994	Tupac is acquitted of sodomy and weapons charges but found guilty of sexual abuse.
February 14, 1995	Tupac begins serving his eighteen-month to four-and-one-half year sentence in New York's Rikers Island penitentiary.
April 1, 1995	Tupac's third album entitled, "Me against the World," debuts at No. 1 on Billboard's pop chart fueled by his single, "Dear Mama." The album goes double platinum in 7 months.
May 1995	Tupac marries longtime girlfriend Keisha Morris.
October 1995	Death Row Records CEO Marion "Suge" Knight posts $1.4 million bail to get Tupac out of jail. Tupac immediately flies to Los Angeles to sign a record contract with Death Row and begins work on his fourth solo album entitled, "All Eyez On Me".
February 1996	Stories of Tupac's alleged affair with Faith Evans

(Rapper Biggie Smalls wife) goes public. Faith denies the stories.

February 13, 1996	Tupac's Death Row debut, "All Eyez On Me," becomes raps first double cd to be released.
April 25, 1996	"All Eyez On Me" goes quintuple platinum.
May 1996	Tupac and Snoop Doggie Dogg release "2 of Americaz Most Wanted." In the video caricatures of Biggie Smalls and Sean "Puffy" Combs are punished for setting up Tupac's November 30th shooting.
June 4, 1996	Death Row releases Tupac's "Hit Em Up" single which is a brutal diatribe against Biggie Smalls, Bad Boy, Mobb Deep, and others.
Mid 1996	Tupac works on a film as a detective for Orion's Urban crime thriller "Gang Related."
September 4, 1996	Tupac returns to New York for the MTV Music Video Awards Show in which he gets into a scuffle.
September 7, 1996	Tupac, Suge Knight, and other friends leave the Mike Tyson/Bruce Seldon fight in Las Vegas in Knight's car. Tupac and his associates are later involved in a physical altercation with a man near the hotel's Grand Garden. Afterwards Knight was stopped by police for playing his car stereo too loudly and for not having license plates on his rented vehicle. He was not cited

and was released a few minutes later. Within a few minutes Tupac Shakur is standing through the roof of the rented BMW 750 sedan traveling eastbound on Flamingo Road when he is shot four times in the chest and Knight's head is grazed by shrapnel. They turn the car around and head for the hospital when they are stopped in traffic. Police catch up with them. Tupac and Knight are taken to University Medical Center. Shakur undergoes his first of three surgeries immediately.

September 8, 1996   Knight is released from the hospital. At 6:20 P.M. Shakur undergoes his second operation.

September 9, 1996   Metro Police and about 20 friends of Shakur are in an altercation over what police called a "misunderstanding." Tensions are calmed with the help of a female friend of Shakur's. No one is arrested. Police patrol the outside of the hospital out of concern for a retaliation for the shooting.

September 11, 1996   Knight, accompanied by his attorneys speak, with Metro Police for about an hour.

September 13, 1996   Tupac Amaru Shakur dies from his injuries.

INDEX